MW00893786

Animals as Seen
Through God's Eyes

Animals as Seen Through God's Eyes

A Walk Through the Bible
in Search of the Truth about Animals

Dwila R. Funk

authorHOUSE®

AuthorHouse™ LLC
1663 Liberty Drive
Bloomington, IN 47403
www.authorhouse.com
Phone: 1-800-839-8640

Cover Artwork created by Patricia Graham

Published by AuthorHouse   06/25/2014

ISBN: 978-1-4969-2141-3 (sc)
ISBN: 978-1-4969-2140-6 (hc)
ISBN: 978-1-4969-2139-0 (e)

Library of Congress Control Number: 2014911228

Any people depicted in stock imagery provided by Thinkstock are models,
and such images are being used for illustrative purposes only.
Certain stock imagery © Thinkstock.

This book is printed on acid-free paper.

Scripture quotations marked KJV are from the Holy Bible, King James Version
(Authorized Version). First published in 1611. Quoted from the KJV Classic
Reference Bible, Copyright © 1983 by The Zondervan Corporation.

Scripture quotations marked NIV are taken from the Holy Bible, New
International Version®. NIV®. Copyright © 1973, 1978, 1984 by International
Bible Society. Used by permission of Zondervan. All rights reserved. [Biblica]

This book is dedicated to Jesus Christ, my Lord and Savior, who nudged me onward and never allowed me to give up on this. It is also dedicated to Marsha Smith, whom God used as a catalyst to start me on this road of discovery of God's plan for all animals. This is also dedicated to all animal lovers who yearn for the truth and all my dear friends who encouraged me along the way. A special thanks to my mom and pop, Loris and Gordon Baustian, who always believed in me, and to all my furry babies. I have been blessed and honored to be a part of their lives. And of course a very special dedication to my Noah, my sweet cocker spaniel that God blessed me with as an answer to a prayer and in whose eyes I saw the eyes of God.

Contents

Foreword

As you will read in this wonderful book, done with a lot of love and research, from the heart, Dwila is a devoted protector and rescuer of all animals, great and small, and people too! She has a profound faith in God and lives her life daily according to God's word.

This book is dedicated to Dwila's dear kiddos and also to others who have been privileged to be a part of Dwila's life. All of us should be dedicating this book to Dwila for her unending love of all animals. She will never stop caring, protecting, and rescuing all of God's creatures. We salute you, Dwila, for all you do! What an adventure you have opened up to all who are fortunate enough to read your book.

Have fun!

—Marsha Smith

Thumper's Gift

This was a story I wrote before I really started walking on the path God was luring me down. Shortly after I moved to the country, I had taken in a couple of orphaned baby cottontail rabbits to raise. This was my first experience raising baby animals. I had to learn a lot to raise these babies, from bottle feeding to caressing them with a warm, damp wash rag to promote relaxation in order for them to do their business. It was a new and wonderful experience. When one of my rabbits died suddenly, I was overwhelmed with grief. I wrote this story, "Thumper's Gift," about a month after her death. It was a way for me to work through the grief and pain. When I was writing the story, a dream I had approximately six months before came to my mind. That dream became intertwined with the story and became its focal point. Looking back on it now, I can clearly see God in all of it. God and His salvation were there all along, hidden in the landscape.

I was mourning the loss of my dear, sweet Thumper. Thumper was a sweet, gentle rabbit that I was blessed with for two-and-a-half years. One winter Saturday in December (which happened to be my birthday), Thumper began to act odd, and I could tell something was terribly wrong. I picked her up to comfort her in my arms, which is where she died. God took my sweet Thumper away as quickly as he had blessed me with her. This had to be one of the worst times in my life, for you see, she was my child in every sense of the word. All of my children, whether their skin is covered with fur or feathers, are my children. Very few people understand this, and many people probably think I am quite an eccentric woman. I feel blessed to have the job of adoptive mother to some of God's most wonderful creatures. They have given me so much and have taught me some of the most valuable lessons about life.

So as you can see, God taking Thumper away was quite devastating to me. And then the question came: "Where did she go? What happened to her soul?" Of course I believe in heaven for all God's creatures, great and small. I also know not everyone shares my view on this. I have heard the view from many people that only human beings are able to enter the kingdom of heaven. Animals are just animals. When they die, they are just dead. End of story. You can probably tell that this would trouble me deeply. I have seen much evil in this world, and the evil has come from man. I have also seen great beauty and grace. This I have seen from nature and animals. Animals are born perfect, full of love, wisdom, and compassion. I know I have been blessed to have the opportunity to experience this in my lifetime. For this, I am truly grateful. I have the utmost respect for animals. I cannot say the same about man. I love this quote by Andy Rooney that I found on some calendar I had: "The average dog is a nicer person than the average person." I definitely agree with that statement.

My grief was great, and this dilemma made it worse. Not only did I fear what had happened to my Thumper but also what would happen to all of my animal children when their time came. I prayed to God for wisdom, for an answer, for a sign. I remember hearing in my head, "Thumper will live forever, because you loved her." What did this mean? And was this voice from God or just me? Or was I just becoming psychotic?

Long nights turned into days; then weeks and months passed. Corey, my little albino parakeet, had grown old and also passed away. I laid her body to rest in the graveyard near Thumper by the edge of my woods. It is a peaceful place where the trees bow over their graves. I go out there often to sit and listen to the sounds of the woods. I talk with God. And I also talk to Thumper and Corey. I know their souls are not there, but I do this anyway. I ponder what has happened to them, and then the grief surfaces all over again. I don't know if you ever truly get over a grief that has wounded you deep down to the very essence of your soul.

One summer night in June, I woke up from a dream about Thumper. I missed her so much that my heart ached. I got up from my bed and peered out a window that looked out over my backyard. The moon was bright. It seemed to cast a halo over the meadow. I could see the tombstones in the graveyard by the woods. With the moon shining down, it appeared as if they were glowing. I knew it was silly, but I was compelled to go out there. I walked quietly to the back door, being mindful not to wake my dogs. I unlocked the door and very carefully opened it, being as quiet as possible, and escaped into the backyard. As I walked carefully toward the back fence by the woods (I wanted to avoid stepping in doggie doo-doo), I realized I had forgotten to put my shoes on and could feel the dew on my feet. I also realized that I had forgotten to put on my robe and that I was outside with only my night shirt. Although it was a summer night, the air was crisp and cool. As I walked toward the edge of the woods, I saw little rabbits playing in the meadow. They were chasing each other around the trees and playing a game of leapfrog. I stopped for a few seconds to watch them play. A smile came to my face and then slowly disappeared as my heart ached for Thumper. I proceeded with my journey to the edge of the woods.

When I finally arrived at the tiny graves, I looked down upon them. "Oh, I miss you so." I wiped a tear from my eye. "Oh God, please let Thumper and Corey be with you. Please let them have a purpose in your kingdom. They were so gentle, so kind, so loving. I know they must have a greater purpose than to live ... die ... that's it." Tears rolled down my face.

Just then, a little rabbit approached me. She came right up to me with great determination. I froze, for you see, she looked and behaved just like Thumper. She came up to my feet and smelled and kissed them gently. Then she sat up on her hind legs and looked up at me as if she were trying to say something. I very slowly lowered myself to my knees, offered my hand for her to smell. She responded to the offering and then allowed me to stroke her fur.

I could feel the tears welling up within me, and then I heard this gentle voice say, "Don't be afraid. It is your beloved Thumper." I swiftly looked up to see a huge brown bear standing before me at the edge of the woods by the graves. Now, this part will sound silly, but I can only tell you how I remember it. This big brown bear was wearing a baby blue, yellow, and white plaid jacket along with a baby blue hat with a small yellow and white feather. He also was carrying a brown briefcase. He lifted up his briefcase and carefully opened it. Reaching in one of the compartments, he removed some yogurt-covered raisins and a few peanuts and almonds. He then offered his paw to me with the treats to take. "Here, I know you would like to give Thumper some treats, and she told me these were her favorites." This was true, for these were the treats I used to give Thumper. She would eat them right out of my hand.

The tears welled up in my eyes as I took the treats from the bear's paw. I lowered myself down on the ground, extended my hand to Thumper, and opened my fingers for her to see what I had. She hopped over to my hand and selected a yogurt-covered raisin. She ate it, savoring every bite. She then returned to my hand and decided to try an almond. Again she ate it, enjoying every nibble. After she ate all the treats, she kissed my fingers and then jumped around twitching her bottom. She then hopped toward the big brown bear. He knelt down, and she jumped up into his arms. He stood back up and gently cradled her in his arm, stroking her fur lovingly. All I could do was stand there, speechless, with tears rolling down my face. I felt as if I were in some kind of a crazy dream. Finally, my mouth was able to form words, but my voice could only manage a whisper. "Who are you? Is this a dream?"

"My name is Mr. Purdue, and no, this is not a dream." His voice, gentle and soothing, seemed to whisper like a soft breeze through the trees.

At this point I realized that he had a white parakeet sitting on his right shoulder. It was Corey. Again my mouth attempted to form words, but all that would come out was a small whisper of a question: "Mr. Purdue?"

His eyes looked at me with such gentle kindness. I had this overwhelming sense of peace pour over me. "I can see this is hard for you. Please don't fear. Be in peace. I am an angel sent by God. God heard your prayers and felt your pain. He sent me—sent us—to ease your suffering." He paused for a moment, stroked Thumper's fur, and then returned his gaze to me. "I am the angel for animals. God so loves them, and He has a very special place for them in His kingdom. Not all know about it. You do now, and you must spread the word. Fear not, for He takes care of all. Look." At this point, he motioned with his paw for me to turn my attention toward the woods. I saw rustling between the trees. I attempted to wipe the tears away and focus my eyes on the woods. You may not believe what I am about to tell you, and to this day, I am still in awe. I gazed upon all kinds of creatures great and small. I saw deer, squirrels, and birds of every kind. I saw wolves, coyotes, dogs, cats, raccoons, opossums, mice, and moles. I saw monkeys, giraffes, zebras, lions, tigers, and even a couple of elephants. There were horses, mules, donkeys, and sheep. I saw rabbits jumping around playing their rabbit games. In spite of seeing the wide range of animals from the smallest and meekest to the mightiest and fiercest, there was no violence, no preying, and no fear. They were eating, resting, playing, and loving. I rubbed my eyes again. I pinched my arm to see if I was dreaming. Mr. Purdue could see I was questioning my senses.

"You are not dreaming. You have been given a great gift. You have been given the gift of seeing the Master's kingdom for animals. None will want. None will feel hunger or pain or sorrow. I am truly sorry for the loss you have felt, but you can now see you have not lost. Thumper is a gentle soul, loving and kind. And you know yourself that she has a great intellect and bravery. I needed help overseeing the mighty kingdom. Thumper was called to serve."

Then I heard a soft, gentle whisper. I knew in an instant who was speaking to me. I turned toward Thumper. "Momma, don't be sad. It is wonderful here. I like my new job, and I do it well. Momma, I love you more than words can say. Be at peace, Momma, for this is how it was meant to be." I quietly walked toward them, leaned over, and kissed Thumper on top of her head.

Walking back to the house that night and returning to bed is all a blur. I couldn't tell you how long I was outside nor what time it was when I went back to bed. Everything seemed like some magical dream, and yet I know it happened. I think back on that night often. Sometimes when I'm walking through the woods, I catch a glimpse of that baby blue, yellow, and white plaid jacket. When I see it, I get a warm, peaceful feeling inside, and all I can do is smile.

Introduction

This book was inspired by my love for animals and for all the other people out there that share that same love. It is for all of you that share that same kindred spirit with all of God's creatures that I finally had to face my fears and find the answer to the questions that plagued me for so long. How does God really see animals? Does God's love extend to all of His creatures? And if so, is there a place for them in His kingdom of heaven? Will we be reunited with our furry and feathery friends in heaven? I knew I wasn't alone with all of the questions I had. There are countless others that have been troubled by the cloud of uncertainty regarding this issue. I had to search out the truth. I wanted to see things through God's eyes, so I set out on a walk with God through His word. To say it has been quite an adventure would be a gross understatement. I have been utterly blown away.

In this book, I am sharing my journey and findings with you—the good, the bad, the ugly, and the most beautiful. I feel as if I am opening up my personal journal for everyone to see, but the truth shall set me, you, and everyone free. This is all about truth … no matter what. I knew that this was something that I had to do no matter what fears I stumbled over. I had to compile all that I found and put it in a form that could reach others who were in the same boat as me and who needed this information just like I did.

Besides my personal story, the bulk of most of the chapters is an overwhelming number of scriptures. They are all written out and are the majority of the content of this book. The reason I did it this way is that this was the kind of book I was searching for. I wanted to find the facts, and I wanted evidence from God's word, the Bible, to support the findings.

Let me give a word of warning. This book is about animals and a tribute to them. It is about how God views animals. This is not a warm, fuzzy book regarding humans. In fact, at times it is quite harsh toward the human condition. When I set out on this mission, I had no idea where it would lead me. I depended on God to show me the way through His scriptures, and He did. What I found in God's word was so much more than I ever expected. To be quite honest, I was completely shocked by what was revealed.

Trust me, the journey is hard at times and even painful, but the final destination is beautiful and wonderful. God is a much bigger God than we can ever imagine. He truly does have everything worked out. He does give each one of us a mission, though, while we are here on Planet Earth. Part of my mission was to compile all the information He has shown me and share it with you. I pray that reading this book will move you, comfort you, and change you. I pray that you will be able to see the big picture through God's eyes and will be inspired to make a difference for God, and then I will pass the torch to you. What will you do with it?

My Journey

It is hard to think of where to begin, but I think for the purpose of what I want to share I need to start back in 1999. It is hard to figure out a beginning point. One event was preceded by a series of previous events that had an impact on the road I am on now. I have to start somewhere, so I am going to plunge in and start. I had a dream. It was almost as if I wasn't dreaming. I remember it took place at night. I dreamed I had walked outside near the edge of my woods. In the woods I saw all kinds of animals. Wild animals, domesticated animals—you name it, it was out there. I then remember a bear walking upright like a person. He was dressed in clothes and carrying a briefcase. (I know this sounds bizarre, but you know how dreams can be!) He came to the edge of the woods and talked with me. I can't remember all that he said. I do remember going back inside and somehow realizing that this was very important. I needed to remember it. It had some significant meaning.

In December of that year, one of my rabbits died suddenly. I had found the rabbits as orphaned babies. I took them in and raised them. Losing Thumper was very hard. It was devastating. A month later, for some odd reason I decided to write a story. I was not a writer, but I had a strong compulsion to write, so I did. The dream I had about the animals in the woods came back to me. When I wrote the story "Thumper's Gift," the dream I had six months earlier became intertwined with the story. It seemed the words came without any control of my own. Writing the story seemed to have a healing quality for me in dealing with my grief over Thumper's death. I shared it with a few people, but beyond that, I did nothing else with it. You see, I still had this nagging question within me. Was there any truth to this? Did animals go to Heaven? Would I ever see my dear friends again? I wanted to know the truth, yet there was a part of me that was afraid to find out.

Now might be a good time to explain a little about where I was on my spiritual path. I have always believed in God, but I really had no knowledge of Him. My family of origin were not church people. We didn't even really talk about God in my family. My maternal grandmother was a strong Christian lady. I credit her for stirring that fire in me about God. She gave me a Bible when I graduated from high school, and I have kept it with me all these years. But the truth be known, I had never read the Bible except for Psalm 23, which I read at the funeral when one of my pets died. I think I was always somehow intimidated by the Bible. I thought I would not understand it, as if you had to go to seminary before you could truly understand what is written in the Bible. I was very ignorant. I didn't know any of the stories in the Bible. I didn't know who the characters were in the Bible. In fact, to be quite honest, I didn't really know what the Bible was all about. Sad, huh? So you can maybe understand why I was a little afraid to know the truth about animals going to heaven. I wasn't sure about God's view on the matter. Oh sure, I know I have the right to believe whatever I want to believe. But just because I choose to believe something doesn't make it the truth. I have always wanted to know the truth about things. Make-believe has never been my strong suit.

I met a woman at work. I remember her asking me a question that really threw me for a loop. She asked, "Are you a Christian?" I wasn't really sure how to respond. I mean, sure, I believed in God. I believed in Jesus, although I don't think at that time I really knew who He was. I had gone to church and finally had been baptized when I joined a church in the city. I really hadn't gone to church much since I moved to the country. The most troubling thing about what she asked was that I didn't really know what being a Christian meant. We ended up having many long talks. I found out that she had actually read the entire Bible! I mean, sure, some people have probably read parts of the Bible, but I couldn't fathom anyone actually reading the entire Bible cover to cover. Was that even possible? She told me it was important to read the Bible for yourself. "Don't just let people tell you what is in it," she told me. "They can lead you astray. You need to be familiar with it yourself." This intrigued me.

The word of God was opened up to me. I prayed for understanding, and I started reading the Bible. Once I started reading, it was hard for me to put the book down. I was like a sponge soaking up every drop. Many things started to happen then. My relationship with God started to grow. Jesus became real to me—who He really is. I started having a true relationship with Him, which was amazing. The way I prayed and who I was as a person shifted and changed, and I didn't even realize it was taking place. This was definitely having a positive impact. I finally found a small country church to attend. God was working and moving in my life.

In July of 2000, my cocker spaniel, Ashley, got sick and died. She was thirteen. I tried to seek comfort from God, but the same old question continued to surface. Was there a place in heaven for animals? I was growing in my faith in God. He answered a prayer of mine the following year when He brought me another dog. Noah was my miracle from God. God showed Himself to me when He answered that prayer of mine. I had no more doubts about His existence (I have written a story about that miracle that you will read later on). The question now remained: Would I trust Him for His answer to my question about animals going to heaven? Could I handle the truth? I needed to know, but if the answer was no, could I worship a God who doesn't care for the animals? Would I want to be in a heaven where my best friends were not there? I asked the question, but I really didn't look for the answer. Well, at least not then.

Then in August of 2001 on a Sunday morning I woke up early and was flipping through the channels on the TV. I didn't have cable or a satellite dish, so it didn't take long to flip through all of them. Anyway, I came to a program that apparently was a prerecorded program. It was a call-in program where you could ask the pastor any question about the Bible and he would do his best to answer. A lady called in and asked about whether there would be animals in heaven. Of course, this caught my attention immediately. What would his answer be? He didn't even seem to hesitate on the answer but said yes. He referred to Isaiah 11 and the peaceable kingdom. Of course I went to my Bible, the one my grandmother had given me so many years ago, to look up Isaiah 11. My Bible was definitely being used now. I hope my grandmother was happy. She went to heaven while I was still in college. I read chapter 11 of Isaiah. Sure enough, it was there. All these animals would get along. They wouldn't hurt each other. They wouldn't eat each other. They would lie down together and play together. Then I remembered my dream and my story about Thumper. Was there something to my dream? Had God been trying to speak to me back then? It sure got me thinking. Okay, now I had some proof that God loves animals and that there are animals in heaven. The question I still had was whether *my* animals be in heaven, my best friends. I asked Him to please let me know. No immediate answers came. Time went on.

Spring of 2002 came. I planned to go to a social work conference. There was a cheap conference in Kansas City for social work month. It was close to home, inexpensive contact hours, and free food; what could be better? I wasn't even sure what it was going to be about. I remember praying on my way to the conference, "Lord, let me get something meaningful out of this conference." I know that may sound silly, but I also didn't want to fall asleep during the conference if it was really boring. I had no idea what God had in store for me. The workshop was titled "Welcome to the Twilight Zone." It was on near-death experiences. The lady speaking was a social worker originally from Overland Park, Kansas, (a local) and had had her own near-death experience. She now worked with other people who had had near-death experiences. I want to clarify that she was talking about people who have died, flat-lined, and then have come back to life. This conference was life changing for me. It was as if God was answering so many of my questions so fast. I was overwhelmed. I can't even put it into words. All I can say is that the woman shared about people who have had near-death experiences and encountered their pets in heaven. Was this for real? It inspired me to start reading all I could on the subject.

During this same month, a friend of mine, Marsha, lost her brother. She and her brother loved animals. I remember having a long talk with Marsha. We were talking of death, heaven, and so on. I know it sounds morbid, but when you have lost someone dear to you, you do talk about such things; that becomes really important. I remember her asking me if I really thought that animals go to heaven. She shared with me that she had attended a church service where the minister preached about animals not having souls and said that they would not go to heaven. The first thought I had was to wonder why anyone would see a need to preach on such a thing, but then I heard the distress in her voice. She said she knew that her brother would not be happy in heaven if his furry friends were not up there with him. Automatically, the social work side of me kicked in. I had to help her.

I decided I would research the fate of animals according to God for myself to see what I could find out. Now, you may be thinking that I should have done this a long time ago, and you are right. It seems like I don't necessarily do things for my own needs, but if someone else is in need, I jump to attention. Go figure. By this time I had actually read through the Bible cover to cover. It took me a couple of years, but I actually did it. There is so much to be absorbed. I think I can reread it throughout my lifetime and continue to learn new things from it. It truly is alive.

That was my mission during the summer months when I was off from work. I was going to research what the Bible truly says about animals and heaven. I got an exhaustive concordance of the Bible so I could look up all the scriptures on the subject. Every appropriate scripture I could find, I would write down on index cards (at the time I had no computer). When I did have access to a computer, I searched the Internet to see what I could find on Christianity and animals in heaven. I printed off the articles and read through each one, highlighting important points. I went to bookstores to see what books I could find on the subject, but there weren't many. I found one book, which I ordered through the Internet. The book *Will I See Fido in Heaven? Scriptures Revealing God's Eternal Plan for His Lesser Creatures* by Mary Buddemeyer-Porter, published by Eden Publications, was close to what I was looking for. She had numerous scriptures that revealed God's plan. After reading the book, looking up every scripture that was noted, and continuing to search out all I could on this subject, it started becoming clear to me that yes, animals do have souls and yes, they will be in heaven. I was becoming more excited by every scripture I found. I also wanted to be sure to read everything around each scripture passage. I didn't want to take anything out of context or just try to prove my point. I was on the search for the truth.

Then one day when I was working on this project, God seemed to speak to me, and I realized He was answering the question I had asked Him a long time ago. The truth had been there all along in His Word. I just needed to look. His answer was more abundant than I ever had dreamed. I found that there is quite a lot about animals in the Bible, much more than just about their eternal fate. I have to say that through working on this project, my love for God has grown so deeply. He made everything—every creature. He knows them intimately and loves them dearly. He truly is a God to be worshipped and praised. And above all, I have found my very best friend!

Now What?

When God tells you to do something, it is important that you do it. I happen to procrastinate. That is not a good thing. I had done all of this research. I had read all of the books I could find on the subject. I had searched the Bible for scriptures pertaining to this subject. I had stacks of index cards with scriptures on them: proof that animals have souls, whether there are animals in heaven, God's love for animals, how we are to treat animals, God's relationship with animals, and so on. I felt pretty confident with all the information I had found and that God was leading me down this path. I really believed that God wanted me to do something with all of this information. My thought was that I needed to write a book. That made sense to me. There are very few books on this subject. I know there are other people like me who are concerned about what happens to their furry or feathery friends when they die. This is something I can do for God and for others who may be hurting and need some answers. Well, that was my plan.

Work started back up with the new school year. Being a school social worker, I keep rather busy during the school year. I have a menagerie of animals at home that requires a lot of my time to care for. I think sometimes I was trying to be too much like Noah and the ark (I'm exaggerating slightly). Anyway, there is a list of chores that have to be done every morning and evening that take up a good chunk of my time. Time goes quickly. Bottom line: I didn't do anything with all of the information I had found. The index cards stayed in their stack. My notes stayed in my notebook. All the articles that I read and highlighted stayed in a notebook with dust collecting on all of them. This wasn't God's plan. I had good intentions, but I didn't follow through. Oh, sure, when someone would talk with me about the subject I would freely share about what I had learned. I would search through my cards and show them scriptures that supported my findings, but then I would put them back away and dust would start collecting on them all over again. I am writing all this down now, and I realize how I must have disappointed God. I sure didn't mean to do that. I wouldn't want to do anything to disappoint God, but the fact remains I think I did.

Well, when God speaks to you about doing something, He doesn't give up. He will try other ways to get your attention. He did that with me in February of 2003. One of the teenage girls at church had asked me to share some of the scriptures I had found regarding animals going to heaven. Of course I was willing to share my index cards with scriptures written on each that I have neatly arranged by topic. I said I would bring them to church on Sunday and we could talk about it after church.

I had been attending Sunday school on a fairly regular basis. We were going through the Bible book by book. We all had a lesson guide to help us through. Our Sunday school class was pretty relaxed. We usually got into some interesting discussions. However, lately there had been a new family attending that had changed the dynamics of things. The husband and wife had been attending our Sunday school class. The man was apparently quite a scholar on the Bible. He apparently had gone to seminary, although he was not a pastor. Being very knowledgeable about the Bible, he tended to monopolize our class discussions. On the Sunday that I was supposed to share my index cards with Kate, the teenage girl, our Sunday school lesson was on the book of Job. Now, before I go any further, you have to remember I brought my little box of all my index cards, which I carried neatly in a little bag sitting right beside me on the pew. Okay, now we can continue.

We were studying the book of Job. This man spoke up in an authoritative manner. "You know why God gave Job double the amount of animals and not as many children? Because children are eternal and animals are not!" he answered his own question without allowing anyone else to reply. He had to repeat this point over and over, as if he loved the sound of his voice and his ability to share his wealth of knowledge to all that could hear. My heart was racing. Why couldn't I speak up? I usually was very comfortable speaking up with my new church family. For some reason I couldn't or wouldn't with this man. I had all my index cards with all the supporting scriptures right beside me. I was infuriated with myself. The truth of the matter was I was intimidated by this man who apparently was so educated on the matter. Who was I to speak up and contradict what this man said? Had I gone to seminary school? Was I well educated on the Bible? Oh sure, I had read the Bible (which took me a couple of years to accomplish) and I had researched this topic, and yes, I did think God had spoken to me on the matter (which only made me sound insane), but the fact was I was just a nobody. I was quiet. I didn't stand up for what I believe in, for what God had been revealing to me. This terrible feeling stirred in my gut and wouldn't leave. I couldn't shake it. Needless to say, I didn't stay after church to share my index cards with all the scriptures written on them with Kate. I went home.

That awful feeling inside my gut wouldn't go away. I will be honest with you. The next Sunday I didn't even go to church. I couldn't face anyone. I couldn't face that man. I felt disgusted with myself. After many sleepless nights and countless talks with God, it hit me that I was also disappointing God. Oh, how I didn't want to do that. God gave me a significant message through scripture:

> For I was an hungered, and ye gave me no meat. I was thirsty, and ye gave me no drink: I was a stranger, and ye took me not in: naked, and ye clothed me not: sick, and in prison, and ye visited me not. Then shall they also answer him, saying, Lord, when saw we thee an hungered, or a thirst, or a stranger, or naked, or sick, or in prison, and did not minister unto thee? Then shall he answer them, saying, Verily I say unto you, In as much as ye did it not to one of the least of these, ye did it not to me. (Matthew 25:42–45, KJV)

If I didn't speak up for animals, which could be considered some of the least of these, was I also not speaking up for Jesus? Mark 8:38 says, "Whosoever therefore shall be ashamed of me and of my words in this adulterous and sinful generation; of him also shall the Son of Man be ashamed, when he cometh in the glory of his Father with the holy angels" (KJV).

By allowing my feelings of intimidation to hold me back from speaking up and sharing what God had revealed to me regarding animals, was I behaving in a way that showed that I was more concerned about what others think than what God thinks? "Therefore to him that knoweth to do good, and doeth it not, to him it is sin" (James 4:17, KJV). That one is the clincher and says it all. I knew what I had to do. Whether I was intimidated or not, I had to face my fears and face this man. God revealed to me that I didn't have to convince this man of anything. I could use this as an opportunity to pick his brain, if you will, about was his view of animals' spiritual fate was founded on. Here was this wonderful opportunity set before me. This man, who was apparently well versed in the Bible and had gone to seminary, could educate me on the basis of people believing animals' fate is not in heaven.

I prayed before entering Church the next Sunday for God to provide the opportunity, the right words, and the courage to follow through. A time presented itself right after Sunday school. God gave me the courage, and I did not hesitate to seize the moment. I went up to him and asked if I could take a moment of his time. I informed him that I had been looking into this issue about animals and would really appreciate if he could share with me where in the Bible he had found that animals do not go to heaven. He gladly shared that in Genesis 2:7, it specifically states, "And the Lord God formed man of the dust of the ground, and breathed into his nostrils the breath of life; and man became a living soul" (KJV).

Okay, I knew about this verse. I had it on one of my index cards (which this time I had left at home). My concern was what else he had. I inquired if there was any other place in the Bible that he used as the basis for this knowledge, and he said no. *No!* I thought. Was that all he had? No other place? I was greatly relieved, and yet more questions surfaced for me. Why do humans take one verse out of the Bible and base all their knowledge of the fate of animals on it without looking at it in the context of verses before and after as well as the rest of the Bible? I was then reminded of how egocentric humans are. They believe everything revolves around them. To think that God cares for other creatures (that He made) doesn't enter their minds. I also realized that if humans truly understood how much God loves animals and His purpose for them and for us and how it was meant to be, humans would be faced with their responsibility to care for animals rather than destroying them. The sad fact is that most humans would rather believe what they have been told and try to make it the truth. But however you cut it, a lie is a lie and a truth is a truth. A lie can never be a truth, and a truth can never be a lie. The human species is the only species that works hard at manipulating information to make it what they want it to be. Animals don't do this. Hmm—we could learn a lot from our fellow creatures.

Back to the Beginning

Let's go back to the beginning and really look at what God says:

> And God said, Let the waters bring forth abundantly the moving creature that hath life, and fowl that may fly above the earth in the open firmament of heaven.

> And God created great whales, and every living creature that moveth, which the waters brought forth abundantly, after their kind, and every winged fowl after his kind: and God saw that it was good.

> And God blessed them, saying, Be fruitful, and multiply, and fill the waters in the seas and let fowl multiply in the earth. And the evening and the morning were the fifth day.

> And God said, Let the earth bring forth the living creature after his kind, cattle, and creeping thing, and beast of the earth after his kind: and it was so.

> And God made the beast of the earth after his kind, and every thing that creepeth upon the earth after his kind and God saw that it was good.

And God said, Let us make man in our image, after our likeness: and let them have dominion over the fish of the sea, and over the fowl of the air, and over the cattle, and over all the earth, and over every creeping thing that creepeth upon the earth. So God created man in his own image, in the image of God created he him; male and female created he them. And God blessed them, and God said unto them, Be fruitful, and multiply, and replenish the earth, and subdue it: and have dominion over the fish of the sea, and over the fowl of the air, and over every living thing that moveth upon the earth.

And God said, Behold, I have given you every herb bearing seed, which is upon the face of all the earth, and every tree, in the which is the fruit of a tree yielding seed; to you it shall be for meat. And to every beast of the earth, and to every fowl of the air, and to every thing that creepeth upon the earth, wherein there is life, I have given every green herb for meat: and it was so.

And God saw everything that he had made, and behold, it was very good.

And the evening and the morning were the sixth day. (Genesis 1:20–31 KJV)

According to these verses, it appears that God created all living creatures in the same way. All are living. All can reproduce. All are vegetarian (at least that was the plan in the beginning). God created man and woman to care for the animals, not to destroy them.

Now, let's address the verse that is quoted to make humans eternal and animals not: "And the Lord God formed man of the dust of the ground, and breathed into his nostrils the breath of life; and man became a living soul" (Genesis 2:7, KJV).

Let's now look at what follows:

> And the Lord God took the man, and put him into the Garden of Eden to dress it and to keep it. And the Lord God commanded the man, saying, Of every tree of the garden thou mayest freely eat: But of the tree of the knowledge of good and evil, thou shalt not eat of it: for in the day that thou eatest there of thou shalt surely die.
>
> And the Lord God said, It is not good that man should be alone; I will make him an help meet for him. And out of the ground the Lord God formed every beast of the field, and every fowl of the air, and brought them unto Adam to see what he would call them: and whatsoever Adam called every living creature, that was the name thereof.
>
> And Adam gave names to all cattle, and to the fowl of the air, and to every beast of the field; but for Adam there was not found an help meet for him.
>
> And the Lord God caused a deep sleep to fall upon Adam, and he slept: and he took one of his ribs, and closed up the flesh instead thereof; And the rib, which the Lord God had taken from man, made he a woman, and brought her unto the man.
>
> And Adam said, This is now bone of my bones, and flesh of my flesh: she shall be called Woman, because she was taken out of man. (Genesis 2:15–23, KJV)

According to the scriptures, it appears that the breath of life is what makes a living soul. The scriptures tell us that man and animals were both created out of the dust of the earth. Woman was created from a rib from man, but man was created out of dust, so it makes sense to say woman was made of dust as well. We also have to note that it is not said at this point that God breathed into the nostrils of animals the breath of life, making them living souls. It is also important to note that it doesn't say He didn't. It is not said that God breathed into the nostrils of woman the breath of life, making her a living soul. Because this is omitted, are we to assume that women are not living souls? That would be absolutely absurd.

I have to take a moment to share something. When I was doing my research and noticed the omission of any statement that the breath of life was breathed into woman's nostrils, making her a living soul, I sarcastically thought to myself, "I guess women aren't living souls either!" I assumed no one would ever think such a ridiculous thing. I didn't realize how wrong I was. It is always amazing to me the way God wants to interact with each one of us. He passionately wants to reveal Himself to us if we can keep our eyes and ears open to hear the still, small voice of God. During the time I was working on this, I happened to read a book called *God's Generals II: The Roaring Reformers* by Robert Liardon. In one of the chapters he mentioned that some believed that women didn't have souls![1] I know I was being sarcastic regarding this very subject, but I had no idea anyone would ever think this to be true. I couldn't believe what I was reading, but then there was this part of me wondering if God was trying to show me something. During this same time, I watched one of my mom's old taped movies

---

[1] Robert Liardon, *God's Generals II: The Roaring Reformers* (New Kensington: Whitaker Houser, 2003) 351–352.

that I hadn't seen before. The movie was set in the 1920s. There were a couple of statements about the belief that women do not have souls. I was absolutely astounded by the repetition of this belief and how crazy it was. This distorted belief has historically been applied to others besides women. I don't know if I have just become more sensitive to this subject or what. I noticed a similar belief being portrayed in some old movies and television programs (old westerns and such) that made reference to people of different races not being human or not having souls, such as America Indians and African Americans. I don't know if this was just a primitive American belief or if this crazy thought had any roots in other countries. I was appalled that anyone would ever consider thinking such a thing. Then it occurred to me that God was trying to let me know that people have believed in lies in the past and believed they had truth. Some of the lies finally have been revealed through the light of the truth. We no longer hear these past beliefs. People know the truth. God let me see that the same will be true with animals. Light will shine on the truth.

From what we have learned so far, do we really have enough information to confidently say that only humans have the breath of life, making them living souls and thus eternal while animals do not share this same fate? I don't know about you, but for me, I'm not convinced. I have heard that the Bible will explain itself. You have to look through the Bible and really read it. Look for patterns—things that are repeated—and find what is consistent. The Bible will define itself. Let's look deeper in the Bible to see what God's word really says on the matter.

We all remember the Bible story of Noah and the ark. I always found it interesting that God put a lot of energy and planning into saving the animals from the flood. I mean, think about all the work He had Noah and his family had to do to make this huge boat that would be able to house all of the animals and Noah's family comfortably. Plus, Noah and his family had to take care of all these animals during the time they spent inside the ark. Well, I'm getting a little off track. Let's get back to the subject. We know the breath of life seems to be equivalent to a living soul. Let's search for some scriptures that talk about the breath of life and the soul.

Genesis 7:15 says, "And they went in unto Noah into the ark, two and two of all flesh, *wherein is the breath of life*" (KJV, emphasis added).

Okay, now let's keep this straight: the breath of life is equivalent to a living soul. That is what we found out in chapter 2 in the verse quoted to support the ideas that humans have living souls and thus are eternal. We have only gone five chapters further in Genesis to get to the story of Noah. God is having animals of every kind board the ark. It precisely says in black and white that these animals were "of all flesh, wherein is the breath of life." Now we know he is talking about the animals. We also know the breath of life signifies a living soul. The passage we read clearly states that animals have the breath of life. I don't think it takes a rocket scientist to figure this one out. If animals have the breath of life, then I can be pretty confident in saying that they have living souls. If you don't believe me, go check it out yourself. In fact, I strongly encourage you to. I also want to add that this phrase, "the breath of life," is used three different times in the story about Noah and the Ark. All three times it refers to both humans and animals (Genesis 6:17; 7:15; and 7:22). From what I know about God, He does not lie. And since I know that He doesn't lie, I can safely trust Him at His word.

We aren't going to stop right here. I think we need to press on and see what else we can find. Let's look at another scripture: "And all flesh died that moved upon the earth, both of fowl, and of cattle, and of beast, and of every creeping thing that creepeth upon the earth, and every man: *all in whose nostrils was the breath of life,* of all that was in the dry land, died" (Genesis 7:21–22, KJV, emphasis added). This passage states that all creatures, both humans and animals, that did not board the ark died: "all in whose nostrils was the breath of life." No distinction is made. Let's look at some more.

Job 12:10 says, "In whose hand is the *soul of every living thing,* and the breath of all mankind." Psalm 150:6 commands, "Let *everything that hath breath* praise the Lord. Praise ye the Lord." In Numbers 31:28, we read, "And levy a tribute unto the Lord of the men of war which went out to battle: *One soul of five hundred, both of the persons, and of the beeves, and of the asses, and of the sheep."* And finally, Revelation 16:3 says, "And the second angel poured out his vial upon the sea; and it became as the blood of a dead man: and *every living soul died in the sea."* (Note that I added the emphasis in each of these verses.)

According to these scriptures, it appears that all living creatures, human and animal alike, have the breath of life and thus have living souls. No distinction is made between the two. In fact, in Job 12:10, Numbers 31:28, and Revelation 16:3, it specifically states that animals have souls.

Let's look a little closer at the difference between body, soul, and spirit. According to *Webster's New World Dictionary,* the definition for *body* is "1. the whole physical substance of a human being, animal, or plant 2. the trunk of a human being or animal 3. a corpse."[2] The body is the vehicle we use to get around and that houses our soul. The body is perishable. It will wear out and die: "In the sweat of thy face shalt thou eat bread, till thou return unto the ground; For out of it

---

[2]   *Webster's New World Dictionary,* 4th ed., s.v. "body."

wast thou taken; for dust thou art, and unto dust shalt thou return" (Genesis 3:19, KJV).

The definition for *soul* from *Webster's New World Dictionary* is "1. an entity without material reality, regarded as the spiritual part of a person 2. the moral or emotional nature of a person 3. spiritual or emotional warmth, force, etc. 4. vital or essential part, quality, etc."[3] Another definition of soul I have heard is "mind, will, emotions." Spirit is defined as "1. a) the life principle, esp. in human beings b) SOUL (sense 1) 2. [*also* S-] life, will, thought, etc., regarded as separate from matter 3. a supernatural being, as a ghost or angel."[4]

According to the definitions, both soul and spirit are very similar in nature. Soul appears to be associated with our personality, our individual uniqueness. It is described as "moral or emotional nature." Spirit is our breath. It is what makes us alive. Although the definitions from *Webster's New World Dictionary* link soul and spirit with human beings, let's see what the Bible has to say. As we have already seen, the Bible states that all living creatures have the breath of life. It also states that animals, like humans, have souls. We also have learned that the breath of life is what makes a living soul, so all creatures (animals and humans) are living souls. The way I understand it is that the spirit is the breath of life of God breathing something special into each creature, creating its own unique identity, which is that creature's living soul. Spirit and soul can't be separated except by God. "For the word of God is quick, and powerful, and sharper than any two edged sword, piercing even to the dividing asunder of soul and spirit, and of the joints and marrow, and is a discerner of the thoughts and intent of the heart" (Hebrews 4:12, KJV).

3   Ibid., s.v. "soul."
4   Ibid., s.v. "spirit."

Our physical body is our shell. It will die and return to dust, but our soul/spirit returns to God. Numbers 16:22 says, "And they fell upon their faces, and said, O God, *the God of the spirits of all flesh,* shall one man sin, and wilt thou be wroth with all the congregation?" (KJV, emphasis added).

Psalm 104:24–31 says,

> O Lord, how manifold are thy works! In wisdom hast thou made them all: the earth is full of thy riches. So is this great and wide sea, wherein are things creeping innumerable, both small and great beasts. There go the ships; there is that leviathan, whom thou hast made to play therein. These wait all upon thee; that thou mayest give them their meat in due season. That thou givest them they gather; thou openest thy hand, they are filled with good. Thou hidest thy face, they are troubled; thou takest away their breath, they die, and return to their dust.
>
> Thou sendest forth thy spirit, they are created: and thou renewest the face of the earth. The glory of the Lord shall endure for ever; the Lord shall rejoice in his works. (KJV)

When the breath of any living creature (whether animal or human) is taken away, the body dies. The body returns to dust. The spirit, though, is of God.

In Ecclesiastes, King Solomon, who is known for his great wisdom that was given by God, shares his concerns about humans' lofty perception of themselves:

> I said in mine heart concerning the estate of the sons of men, that God might manifest them, and that they might see that they themselves are beasts. For that which befalleth the sons of

men befalleth beasts; even one thing befalleth them: as the one dieth, so dieth the other; yea, *they have all one breath;* so that a man hath no preeminence above a beast; for all is vanity. All go unto one place; all are of dust, and all turn to dust again. Who knoweth the spirit of man that goeth upward, and the spirit of the beast that goeth downward to the earth? (Ecclesiastes 3:18–21, KJV, emphasis added)

King Solomon, who is known for his great wisdom, clearly asks, "Who really knows that the spirit of man goes upward and the spirit of animals goes downward to the earth?" This shows his concern for the egotistical nature of man.

"Vanity of vanities, saith the Preacher, vanity of vanities; all is vanity" (Ecclesiastes 1:2, KJV). King Solomon states that man's thinking is vain—full of foolishness and emptiness. Man thinks highly of himself yet misses the wisdom of God.

This is a good time for us to travel back to the Garden of Eden and really see what exactly happened there. "And God saw everything that he had made, and, behold, it was very good. And the evening and the morning were the sixth day" (Genesis 1:31, KJV).

In the beginning, after God made everything—after making the heavens and earth; after making mountains and seas; after making all the trees, flowers, and grass; after making all the fish, birds, and animals; after making man and woman—God looked around at everything He made and saw that it was very good. He made it the way He wanted it to be, and He was pleased.

The Garden of Eden was self-sufficient. Adam and Eve had all they needed. Both animals and humans were made vegetarian. God gave the fruit of the trees and herbs of the field to be their food. Therefore, there would be no harm. No one would hurt another living creature. There would be no killing. There would be no want. Man was put in charge to care for all the animals and the land. They were to take care of what God had put them over just as God takes care of all.

So what happened? God gave them herbs to eat and fruit to eat. There was only one condition God put on man and woman: "But of the tree of the knowledge of good and evil, thou shalt not eat of it: For in the day that thou eatest thereof thou shalt surely die" (Genesis 2:17, KJV).

Adam and Eve had everything they could want—a beautiful place to live, good food to eat. The one condition shouldn't have been that hard to keep. It shouldn't have been, but the devil, disguised as the serpent, entered the picture. This was when lies, deceit, and distortion of the truth came into play:

> Now the serpent was more subtle than any beast of the field which the Lord God had made. And he said unto the woman, Yea, hath God said, Ye shall not eat of every tree of the garden? And the woman said unto the serpent, We may eat of the fruit of the trees of the garden: but of the fruit of the tree which is in the midst of the garden, God hath said, Ye shall not eat of it, neither shall ye touch it, lest ye die. And the serpent said unto the woman, ye shall not surely die: For God doth know that in the day ye eat thereof, then your eyes shall be opened, and ye shall be as gods, knowing good and evil. (Genesis3:1–5, KJV)

The devil, using his seductive ways, lured woman into believing that God was wrong; they wouldn't die if they ate the fruit of the tree of knowledge of good and evil. God doesn't lie, but the devil does: "And the great dragon was cast out, that old serpent, called the Devil, and Satan, which deceiveth the whole world: he was cast out into the earth, and his angels were cast out with him" (Revelation 12:9, KJV).

The tempter enticed the desire in humans to be like God—all knowing. Although God had made it clear that the tree of knowledge of good and evil was strictly off limits, woman and man decided that they knew better than God what was good for them and ate of the forbidden fruit. "And when the woman saw that the tree was good for food, and that it was pleasant to the eyes, and a tree to be desired to make one wise, she took of the fruit thereof, and did eat, and gave also unto her husband with her; and he did eat" (Genesis 3:6 KJV).

Because the tempter is a liar and a deceiver, the effect of eating the forbidden fruit was not what the humans expected. "And the eyes of them both were opened, and they knew that they were naked; and they sewed fig leaves together, and made themselves aprons" (Genesis 3:7, KJV). All innocence was gone. The experience wasn't wonderful and enlightening; rather they were left with shame, guilt, and fear.

Now after this happened, you would think (or hope) that they would realize they had made a huge mistake, confess to God what they did, and ask for mercy and forgiveness, but that isn't the action that they took. They hid from God. Sound familiar? Probably if the truth be known, many of us take the same road when we have really screwed up. Instead of being honest and taking ownership for their behavior, both man and woman blamed someone else for their actions—a total lack of responsibility. We really haven't changed much, have we? Too bad we humans can't seem to learn from others' past mistakes. When God confronted man with eating from the tree he had commanded them not to, man blamed woman and ultimately God for his behavior: "And the man said, The woman whom thou gavest to be with me, she gave me of the tree, and I did eat" (Genesis 3:12, KJV). Man blamed woman for his own behavior, but man also blamed God, because it was God who made woman for him.

"And the Lord God said unto the woman, What is this that thou hast done? And the woman said, The serpent beguiled me, and I did eat" (Genesis 3:13, KJV). Woman blamed the serpent for tricking her. Both man and woman blamed others for their own decisions and behavior.

Let's take a closer look at what transpired. Humans had a close relationship with God, at least up until their flagrant disobedience, at which point that relationship was broken. After wanting something they couldn't have (coveting), they took it anyway (trespassing and stealing). Then they hid. When confronted with what they had done, they failed to take responsibility for their actions, blamed someone else for their error in behavior, and attempted to justify their actions due to being misled. Do you see the layers of sin, deceit, and distortion of truth?

Although man and woman did not die physically at that moment, death entered the picture. The life God had planned for them was no longer an option. Pain, sorrow, and hard work were now part of their life until their ultimate death: "In the sweat of thy face shalt thou eat bread, till thou return unto the ground; for out of it wast thou taken: for dust thou art, and unto dust shalt thou return" (Genesis 3:19, KJV).

It appears that God's plan was for a harmonious life. Humans were to care for the land, for the birds, for the fish, and for all the animals. All would live in peace together—a peaceful kingdom. All would commune with God. This all changed when man and woman sinned; going against what God had commanded. They were willing to trust someone else (the serpent) rather than God for what was best for them. Pride, ambition, and selfishness took front stage of their character. Their desire was for unlimited freedom without responsibility. These prideful, self-serving tendencies have been humans' downfall ever since, and all creation has suffered for it.

To save humankind and ultimately all creation, God had to kick man and woman out of the garden before they ate of the tree of life. "And the Lord God said, Behold, the man is become as one of us, to know good and evil: and now, lest he put forth his hand, and take also of the tree of life, and eat, and live forever: Therefore the Lord God sent him forth from the Garden of Eden to till the ground from whence he was taken. So he drove out the man; and he placed at the east of the Garden of Eden Cherubims, and a flaming sword which turned every way, to keep the way of the tree of life" Genesis (3:22–24, KJV).

Can you only image if we lived forever with our sinful ways and were cut off from God with no hope of redemption? The thought horrifies me. Thank the Lord He already had another plan in mind to save us from ourselves and bring us all (creatures included) back to Himself.

The reason I have spent so much time addressing the fall into sin by man and woman is to fully illustrate exactly what the sin was about and how we are still haunted by those same exact characteristics today. Humans, deep down, still believe they are the center of everything. Humans are selfish, self-centered, egocentric creatures. We even go so far as to believe God's love only extends to us humans, even though the Bible gives countless scriptures that provide evidence of His tender love for all creatures and creation. Humans believe that humans alone receive eternal life. Please take a moment and ponder this. Can humans be any more self-centered and self-serving?

I believe it is this ingrained self-centered, self-serving nature in us that is the basis for the distortion of truth and outright lies that have been passed on from generation to generation. When a lie is told over and over, people begin to believe the lie is truth. Remember, though, that a lie can never be a truth no matter how you wrap it.

"The heart is deceitful above all things, and desperately wicked: who can know it?" (Jeremiah 17:9, KJV).

After the Fall

After the fall of man into sin, Adam and Eve were kicked out of the Garden of Eden. Sin still lurked in their midst. We have heard of their children, Cain and Abel. Cain was jealous of Abel and killed him. God gave Adam and Eve another son, Seth. Seth had a son, Enos, and "then began men to call upon the name of the Lord" (Genesis 4:26, KJV).

It was through this seed that the chosen people of God came to be. Through this seed came Noah. I am going to walk you through this entire story. There are many things that transpired. It is important to look at every part. Initially, I planned to break it up and cover the different parts in separate chapters. It then occurred to me that it made more sense to keep it all in context and cover all the parts in one chapter.

Sin and wickedness had spread throughout the land. God looked at His creation and was sickened by what He saw. "And God saw that the wickedness of man was great in the earth, and that every imagination of the thoughts of his heart was only evil continually" (Genesis 6:5, KJV).

God was saddened that what He had made had been corrupted. He had serious thoughts about destroying everything He had created here. "And it repented the Lord that he had made man on the earth, and it grieved him at his heart. And the Lord said, I will destroy man whom I have created from the face of the earth; both man, and beast, and the creeping thing, and the fowls of the air; for it repenteth me that I have made them" (Genesis 6:6–7, KJV).

Now think about this: God was very upset with what was happening here. He was so upset that He seriously considered pitching the whole thing! But God saw Noah and saw something different in this man. "But Noah found grace in the eyes of the Lord. These are the generations of Noah: Noah was a just man and perfect in his generations, and Noah walked with God"(Genesis 6:8–9, KJV).

God talked with Noah and informed him of what He planned to do. "The earth also was corrupt before God, and the earth was filled with violence. And God looked upon the earth, and, behold, it was corrupt; for all flesh had corrupted his way upon the earth. And God said unto Noah, The end of all flesh is come before me; for the earth is filled with violence through them; and, behold, I will destroy them with the earth" (Genesis 6:11–13, KJV).

God instructed Noah to build an ark. He told him exactly how to build it (Genesis 6:14–16). God then shared with Noah the rest of His plan:

> And, behold, I, even I, do bring a flood of waters upon the earth, to destroy all flesh, wherein is the breath of life, from under heaven; and every thing that is in the earth shall die. But with thee will I establish my covenant; and thou shalt come into the ark, thou, and thy sons, and thy wife, and thy sons' wives with thee. And of every living thing of all flesh, two of every sort shalt thou bring into the ark, to keep them alive with thee; they shall be male and female. Of fowls after their kind, and of

cattle after their kind, of every creeping thing of the earth after his kind, two of every sort shall come unto thee, to keep them alive. And take thou unto thee of all food that is eaten, and thou shalt gather it to thee; and it shall be for food for thee, and for them. Thus did Noah; according to all that God commanded him, so did he. (Genesis 6:17–22, KJV)

God decided to save Noah and his family and also two of each living creature of the earth from the destruction He had planned. Not only did God save a remnant of humans through Noah's family, but He also wanted to preserve a remnant of all living creatures. Both humans and all creatures have the breath of life.

There is another point that I need to share. It will be important for us to discuss later on. We will come back to it. "Of every clean beast thou shalt take to thee by sevens, the male and his female: and of beasts that are not clean by two, the male and his female. Of fowls also of the air by sevens, the male and the female; to keep seed alive upon the face of all the earth" (Genesis 7:2–3, KJV).

There are some important messages that we can get from these scriptures. First of all, God cares for humans and wanted to save them through Noah and his family. He also cares deeply for all His creatures and wanted to save a remnant of them as well. That is why He instructed Noah to get two of each kind, both male and female. He wanted them to replenish the earth. He instructed Noah on supplies that he would need, including food for Noah's family and for all the creatures. God wanted Noah to take care of all the animals, including birds and all creeping animals. Noah was to be their caretaker. All ate food from the land. Noah was to be sure to get enough food for all to eat in the ark. It is important not to miss these points. God explained His expectations for caring for His creatures. They are important to Him. If that were not so, He would have told us that in the Bible, but instead He speaks very clearly of His desires.

Another important point to look at is how overwhelming this task that God requested from Noah must have seemed to be! Now, I don't know about you, but when I ponder this point, I am astounded when I try to imagine exactly how Noah accomplished such a project. How did he get all these animals, birds, and all creeping things to come with him and board the ark? That would not be an easy task. Plus, I highly doubt that all those animals, birds, and creeping things lived close to Noah in his own neighborhood. Would he even have known where to look for them? He also had to make sure he got both male and female. Now with some animals it is easy to tell what sex they are, and the sex of some birds can be distinguished by the different coloring of their feathers, but I know there are some animals and birds whose sex is not so easy to identify. How was Noah able to accomplish such a task? If we look at the next verses, God says, "For yet seven days, and I will cause it to rain upon the earth forty days and forty nights; and every living substance that I have made will I destroy from off the face of the earth. And Noah did according unto all that the Lord commanded" (Genesis 7:4–5, KJV).

It doesn't sound like Noah had tons of time to gather all the animals and board the ark. Granted, who knows for sure exactly how the time went. Verse 7:7 states that Noah and his family went into the ark. Verses 7:8–9 state that all the animals, all the fowl, and all the things that creep on the earth entered the ark as God commanded. Then again in 7:14–16 it states, "They, and every beast after his kind, and all the cattle after their kind, and every creeping thing that creepeth upon the earth after his kind, and every fowl after his kind, every bird of every sort. And they went in unto Noah into the ark, two and two of all flesh, wherein is the breath of life.

And they that went in, went in male and female of all flesh, as God had commanded him: and the Lord shut him in" (Genesis 7:14–16, KJV).

Because God commanded all of this, it makes sense to me that He Himself called the animals to come to Noah and enter the ark. It doesn't really say how it all came about but that everything was done as God commanded it. That would mean that all these animals, little critters, and all the birds heard God's voice and did what He told them to do. Even if Noah and his sons had to go look for any of the animals and birds, the animals and birds still had to be willing to go with them. Another thing to think about is the fact that Noah's family and all these animals were going to be living together for quite a while. None of them harmed each other (people or animals) during their entire stay on the ark. There was enough food for everyone. To me, that is a huge miracle in itself. God facilitated it so that it would happen according to His plan.

Then the rain began and the waters rose. The flood was for forty days. This was a flood that surpasses our wildest imagination. Everything outside of the ark died. There was no chance for anything to survive.

> And all flesh died that moved upon the earth, both of fowl, and of cattle, and of beast, and every creeping thing that creepeth upon the earth, and every man: All in whose nostrils was the breath of life, of all that was in the dry land, died. And every living substance was destroyed which was upon the face of the ground, both man, and cattle, and the creeping things, and the fowl of the heaven; and they were destroyed from the earth: and Noah only remained alive, and they that were with him in the ark. And the waters prevailed upon the earth an hundred and fifty days. (Genesis 7:21–24, KJV)

God purged the land with the flood. All the wickedness was washed away. "And God remembered Noah, and every living thing, and all the cattle that was with him in the ark: and God made a wind to pass over the earth, and the waters asswaged; The fountains also of the deep and windows of heaven was restrained; And the waters returned from off the earth continually: and after the end of the hundred and fifty days the waters were abated" (Genesis 8:1–3, KJV).

Just a quick side note I want to add here: I watched a program on television that focused on the discovery of Noah's ark. Apparently it has been discovered nestled up on Mount Ararat in Turkey. Why would there be any question of where it is located? Look at the next verse: "And the ark rested in the seventh month, on the seventeenth day of the month, upon the mountains of Ararat" (Genesis 8:4, KJV).

After the waters subsided, God told Noah that he and everyone with him could leave the ark. They were to go out and replenish the earth. Now, several things happened here that we need to be aware of. First of all, remember that Noah was instructed by God to bring seven of certain animals and birds? God knew ahead of time what Noah would do. Once Noah left the ark, he built an altar to the Lord, taking some of those animals and birds (which were brought on the ark by sevens) and offered burnt offerings on the altar (Genesis 8:20). God did not ask for him to do this, but I am sure God knew this would happen. Knowing this, God had Noah bring extra of some animals and birds. If He hadn't, no doubt Noah would have killed some of the animals, losing those species forever, for they wouldn't have had a chance to reproduce, replenishing the earth.

"And the Lord smelled a sweet savour; and the Lord said in his heart, I will not again curse the ground any more for man's sake; *for the imagination of man's heart is evil from his youth;* neither will I again smite any more every thing, as I have done" (Genesis 8:21, KJV, emphasis added).

Reading this scripture bothered me at first. I do not feel good about animal sacrifices. But after reading it several times, I started to see the whole message. It isn't that God likes animal sacrifices; He made these beautiful creatures, and He doesn't want any one of them to suffer needlessly. God maybe saw what the true condition of the world really was. God didn't rid the earth of all evil. Sin would still remain. Even though God saw good in Noah, Noah was still human and "the imagination of man's heart is evil from his youth." As long as humans still live on this earth, the stain of sin remains.

Everything on the earth was changed. This leads us to changes in relationships. No longer would animals and humans be friends together. A disconnection happened. This is one of the major changes that took place. The next major change is that God gave Noah and his family permission to use the animals for food. We have to remember that the earth had been flooded. Anyone who has experienced a devastating flood can attest to the fact that the vegetation would have been destroyed. Noah and his family were probably about out of food. God gave them permission to use animals as food just as He has given them all the vegetation for food. I highly doubt God wanted humans to use flesh as their main source of nourishment. Once vegetation was regained, I am sure God would have hoped that humans would go back to their original state, being primarily vegetarian. Of course, we know that didn't happen.

"And the fear of you and the dread of you shall be upon every beast of the earth, and upon every fowl of the air, upon all that moveth upon the earth, and upon all the fishes of the sea; into your hand are they delivered. Every moving thing that liveth shall be meat for you; even as the green herb have I given you all things" (Genesis 9:2–3, KJV).

Animals of all kinds, fish of the waters, and birds of the air all suffered because of humans' sin. There would be no peace on earth. Animals also changed from their original state. Some of the animals, who were once peaceful and loving, now became like savages, killing and eating flesh. Other animals became prey to the fiercer ones. And the worst beast of all was man. The earth became a war zone.

It saddens me deeply to see what happened. Sometimes I wonder if God wept terribly at how His beautiful creation was so dramatically altered and damaged. Our God, though, is a God of hope. Even though this seems to be such a curse upon all creation, God sent a message of hope. He made a covenant between Himself, Noah and his descendants, and all the animals. A covenant is a solemn agreement, a contract. For God to make a covenant with humans and all animals speaks volumes about God's love for all He made.

> And God spoke unto Noah and to his sons with him, saying, And I, behold, I establish my covenant with you, and with your seed after you; and with *every living creature that is with you, of the fowl, of the cattle, and of every beast of the earth with you; from all that go out of the ark, to every beast of the earth.* And I will establish my covenant with you; *neither shall all flesh be cut off anymore by the waters of a flood;* neither shall there any more be a flood to destroy the earth. And God said, This is the token of the covenant which I make between me and you and *every living creature that is with you,* for perpetual generations: I do set my bow in the cloud, and it shall be for a token of a covenant

between me and the earth. And it shall come to pass, when I bring a cloud over the earth, that the bow shall be seen in the cloud: And I will remember my covenant, which is between me and you and *every living creature of all flesh;* and the waters shall no more become a flood to destroy *all flesh.* And the bow shall be in the cloud; and I will look upon it, that I may remember the everlasting covenant between God and *every living creature of all flesh that is upon the earth.* (Genesis 9:8–16, KJV, emphasis added)

It is very clear that this covenant covers all creation. It is very specific and detailed about this fact. There is no mistake that this covenant is for all of us and all of God's creatures. This covenant gives a promise of good things to come. Further on, I will share other covenants that God will make with humans and animals. Knowing this, I know God was giving a sign of hope for all creation with His sign of the rainbow.

What can we learn from Noah and the ark? For me, this journey has been bittersweet. There is both sadness and joy. God reveals how much He hates the evil in the world and how much He truly loves all of His creation. He provides wisdom and instruction regarding the expectations He has for man. God wants man to take care of all His creatures. Man was created in God's image, and with that comes immense responsibility. Sin still lives in our midst. People still have evil in their hearts. Yet God hasn't given up. He still loves us all. What a love He has! Relationships have changed between man and creatures. They no longer live in the Garden of Eden where peace and joy were overflowing. Death, pain, and sadness have taken a solid stand. Even though a schism took place between humans and animals, God never cut off His communication with any of us. He still reaches out to humans, and He still reaches out and speak to all animals. In the midst of all that transpired, God gave a sign of hope: His covenant with man and all creatures. He gives His beautiful rainbow, which is a beacon in the dark storms of life. Even though the storms of life can seem unbearable, He gives us something beautiful to fix our eyes on. His love—His plan—will see us through. This reminds me of the movie *Because of Winn-Dixie.* If you haven't seen this movie, I would highly recommend it. There is a part in the movie when the little girl, Opal, is reflecting on what she is learning about life. I think sharing this quote is a perfect way to end this chapter: "I thought about how life was like a Littmus Lozenge, how the sweet and sour were all mixed up together, and how hard it was to separate them out."

God's Perfect Plan

My Story about Noah

Ashley was a beautiful buff cocker spaniel. I bought her at a pet store when I was there to adopt a parakeet. My albino parakeet, Ralph, had passed away. I went to buy another bird as a companion for Charli, my other parakeet. In one of the cages in the back of the pet store there was a cute buff cocker spaniel. I walked back to the cages to look at the puppies. Although I had no money, I bought the cocker spaniel girl. She was my first big purchase on my credit card. I know that isn't good to do, but I did it. I named her Ashley Marie. If I was a bit hesitant about making such a decision, it was too late and no turning back. I was hooked. We were so bonded. Ashley taught me so many things. She taught me about love, about forgiveness, about the important things of life, and about myself. She taught me about what real compassion looks like and the true nature of unconditional love.

Four years later I adopted another buff cocker spaniel. Albert was quite different from Ashley. He had been severely neglected. With time, he learned to trust. He fell in love with Ashley the first time he met her. I have to say that Ashley did not quite feel the same way. Albert wouldn't give up and eventually won her over. Those two had such a love for each other and for me. I always would say that Ashley and I were soul mates. We had such a strong connection. She could read me like a book. She could sense my emotions. She knew when I was down and would just sit with me. The sad thing is I could sense something was wrong with her toward the end. Even though I tried to do everything I could, I also didn't want to see what I was seeing. Ashley's time here was coming to a close.

As life is, things could not always stay bright and sunny. Dark days come, and storms blow. Ashley became ill. Her kidneys were starting to fail. I did everything I could. I changed her diet. We had numerous trips to the vet. I prayed nonstop. I so wanted to change the course of this, but as things are not in my control, on July 17, 2000, my sweet, dear Ashley left us. As sweetly as she came into my life, she parted. The pain and anguish is hard to even put into words. Oh sure, I have felt pain in my life before. Life isn't always marshmallows and roses. Sometimes we have real bumpy and rocky roads to go down, but nothing ever prepared me for this. My heart sank to the pit of my stomach. I wasn't alone with this despair. Albert was in pain too. He was hurting with grief due to losing his partner.

Hours turned to days, and days turned to weeks. The pain didn't lighten. I began to believe that I would never feel alive again. I saw a change in Albert. His step was no longer light and cheerful. He had a cloud over him. I began to think I should look into getting another dog for Albert even though I didn't think I could love again. I gave my heart and soul to Ashley. It was Albert I had to be concerned about. What did he need? I prayed to do what was right and for God to show me the way.

I wanted another cocker spaniel. Oh no, I couldn't and wouldn't even try to replace Ashley. That would be impossible. I thought Albert might take to a cocker spaniel better. You have to remember I was not in my right mind. I was still terribly depressed and grief stricken. I saw an ad in the *County Shopper* for two buff cocker spaniels for sale. They were only six weeks old. I called and asked if I could bring my dog along to see if he would take to one. I thought this might be an answer to a prayer. Maybe this was what God was wanting.

The trip was not exactly what I was planning. The two little cocker pups were cute but very whiny. Albert was less than pleased. In fact, I could tell he was very uncomfortable with the situation. I looked into his eyes, and he looked back at me. It was as if I could hear him say, "Please, Mom, don't do this. I can't bear this now." Well, I left with Albert but no puppy. Something overwhelming in me said it wasn't right. I tried again with a puppy that I heard about from the vet. The results were the same. Albert wanted no part of any dog. Albert, who was always friendly with other animals, now seemed unable to tolerate anybody new. I kept trying to fix the situation and find someone for Albert, but all my attempts were failures. After feeling totally defeated and unsure of what the next move should be, I went to God.

"Lord, I need your help. I can't fix this one. I don't know what to do. I don't know if I am to get another dog or not. If it is supposed to be just Albert and me, that is okay. I am tired of trying to fix things. I always mess things up. Lord, I want Your will to be done. But Lord, if we are to get another dog, I want You to bring it to us. I am not going to do anything else without You. If it is Your will, could You bring a dog that needs a good home? And Lord, could it be a cocker spaniel? And could it be buff in color? And Lord, could you have it be that Albert and this dog take to each other and get along great? Lord, I am not going to do anything without You. I need to know that this is about You. So please, if this is Your will, could You put this dog right in front of me so that I know beyond a shadow of a doubt it is from You? I don't want to steal anybody's dog, and I don't want to do anything that is not of You. If this is not Your will, that is okay. I want what You see is best for us. Lord, I am not going to make any move on this. I am going to wait on You. Lord, if you choose to do this, I will sing Your praises and share this miracle with everyone I meet. I will never forget this, and I will tell everyone of Your wonderful love. This is my covenant with You." So that was my prayer. Pretty crazy, huh? Well, that prayer changed my life. It was the first time I prayed and totally turned it over to God. I was totally trusting in Him and His will. Any time I started to think about helping out and taking back control, I immediately turned it right back to God. I could not and would not do anything without God. I couldn't trust myself anymore. I trusted God.

That prayer took place around September of 2000. Time ticked on. I made no moves on my own. I trusted in God and His will. The holidays came and went. Our hearts were still heavy with the loss of Ashley, but we took it a day at a time and went through the motions of everyday life. I didn't think about the prayer much. I had given it to God, and I wasn't worrying about it. Boy, that was a first! Usually I worried about everything. I didn't with this. I knew I was not to make any move. When and if the time came for me to do something, God would let me know. That was that.

Spring came, and nature was waking up from its long winter's nap. Trees were starting to bud. Tulips were in bloom. The air was filled with the scents of spring. Fresh color was filling the countryside as if even Mother Nature wanted to put on a new outfit and pack away the coat and sweaters of winter. It was the middle of May, and I was heading to work. Not even a mile from my house, I saw a buff colored cocker spaniel. He appeared dirty. He was visiting with a neighbor dog and then crossed the street and went off into a field. Believe it or not, I didn't think a whole lot about it. It did register with me that I had seen a cocker spaniel. I live in the country. I see a lot of labs and mutts of various kinds but rarely cocker spaniels. I said a prayer for the dog's safety (as I do with all animals I see) and went on to work.

A few days later I was heading to work again and was running a bit late. This time I saw the little cocker in the street. He was right in front of me. His head was hanging low, and he was walking very slowly. He didn't even realize I was behind him. He looked dirty and unkempt. All of a sudden I heard a voice in my head scream, "Stop! You have to help this dog, or he'll die!" I stopped and went out to the dog. He appeared scared, but he didn't run away. He laid down in the middle of the street and rolled over on his back. He had no collar and was extremely dirty, and his hair was matted all over. He had a cut on his eyelid, which was red and a little bloody. What was even worse, though, was that he was covered literally from head to foot with ticks. Some of the ticks I could tell had been on him a long time. Ticks were having baby ticks. I am telling you I have never seen a worse case. I couldn't leave him there. I had to take care of him and help him find his home, so that's just what I did. I left him outside in the fenced part of my backyard. Albert stayed in the house so I wouldn't worry about any confrontation between them. I gave him food and water and went on to work. I figured I would check around to see if there were any signs posted for a lost cocker spaniel. I still was not thinking this was my dog.

On my way home that evening, I saw him walking up my street. He apparently was able to get out under my fence, which is one of those farm fences that can be bent upward at the bottom fairly easily. His head was hanging low, and he looked so sad. Flies were swarming all over him. I stopped and asked a neighbor boy if he had seen this dog before and if he knew where he lived. He said he had seen him before but didn't know where his home was. The boy helped me get this little guy into my car, and I took him home. I was concerned with all the flies swarming around him and was sure that wasn't a good sign, so I called the vet and took him in. The vet checked him out and gave him something to help with killing the ticks and fleas. Then the vet said, "Dwila, you don't want this dog. He is going to have ear problems just like Ashley did." I just listened to what he said, paid my bill, and took this little boy home with me.

The next challenge would be introducing Albert to this little guy. Now remember, Albert hadn't liked any new dogs since Ashley passed away. I put the little cocker in a pen area I had for my ducks, and I let Albert out. Albert went right up to the fenced area and started barking at the little cocker. The little cocker didn't bark back. In fact, he just sat there, his head hanging low. He looked so sad. I stooped beside Albert and looked him straight in the eye. "Albert, this little guy is hurting. He hasn't been cared for, and he is lonely. He needs a friend. Can you be his friend?" What I saw next was nothing less than amazing. Albert's whole disposition changed. He softened. He went up to the fence, wiggling all over, and was kind to the little cocker. I was able to let the little guy out of the fenced pen so both of them could get to know each other. The connection was immediate. I stood and watched in amazement. Albert, who had been hardened and sad, softened and became like a pup again. The little cocker took to Albert quickly. It was like he finally had a family and a friend of his own.

I spent about a week picking off all the ticks by hand. There really isn't any other way. He got a bath and a haircut. He looked like a new dog. I named him Noah. There were never any signs posted for a lost cocker spaniel. No one seemed to know whom he belonged to. So on May 22, 2001, God answered my crazy prayer. It took me a while to realize that God had indeed answered my prayer. He had given me a buff-colored cocker spaniel who was definitely in need of care, who needed a home, who was placed right in front of me, and who took to Albert and Albert to him. This is a true story, and none of this was made up to sound better. It is the whole truth and nothing but the truth, so help me God. I know beyond a shadow of a doubt that God answered my prayer. God took mercy on me and my situation. Life was breathed into us again. There is no question in me, no doubt, that God is real. He listens to us.

He loves us and all His creatures. In all my despair, I was never alone. God had a plan all along. He brought me Noah and showed me that I could love again. Noah is the sweetest, gentlest dog. He was looking for a home, a family, and a place where he would be loved. We were in need of healing. God brought us all together so we all could mend. Noah now has a family where he is dearly loved. My heart has grown even bigger with the love I feel for him. He is my wonderful gift from Jesus, and I think Ashley gave him a big kiss before she sent him my way. I have upheld my promise to God. I tell everybody I meet about God's wonderful love and my miracle of Noah.

Let's Sing Praises
to the Lord, for He Is Good

God has never cut off His ties with humans and animals. He continues to reach out to all of His creation. Because humans were made in the image of God, they were given free will. They can choose to obey God or not. They can choose to worship God or not. Animals were not made that way. They know who their Maker is and worship Him. The Bible rings very clear on the subject of how all creatures praise the Lord. The Psalms are full of examples of their praises. The scriptures also share numerous ways God cares for all He made, both creatures and all creation. Many of the scriptures intertwine both of these messages together. These scriptures provide me with peace, hope, and more of a reason to praise the Lord for how awesome He truly is. It may be quite easy for a person to say, "Oh, that is just pretty poetry. It isn't real." Well, my response is either the Bible is the word of God and truthful or it isn't. It can't be both. There is no in between. Let us take a look at a few examples. Because there are so many, I can't put them all down. I will share several though. Please make note of the consistency of the message. It is like a dance with God Almighty. His heart is pure and loving. He does nothing without a reason. Let us embrace the message and take a closer walk with our God.

2 Kings 3:17 says, "For thus saith the Lord, Ye shall not see wind, neither shall ye see rain; yet that valley shall be filled with water, that ye may drink, both ye, and your cattle, and your beasts" (KJV).

1 Chronicles 16:30–34 says, "Fear before him, all the earth: the world also shall be stable, that it be not moved. Let the heaven be glad, and let the earth rejoice: and let men say among the nations, The Lord reigneth. Let the sea roar, and the fullness thereof: let the fields rejoice, and all that is therein. Then shall the trees of the wood sing out at the presence of the Lord, because he cometh to judge the earth. O give thanks unto the Lord; for he is good; for his mercy endureth forever" (KJV).

Here is Nehemiah 9:6: "Thou, even thou art Lord alone; thou hast made heaven, the heaven of heavens, with all their host, the earth, and all things that are therein, the seas, and all that is therein, and thou preservest them all; and host of heaven worshippeth thee" (KJV).

"Thy mercy, O Lord, is in the heavens; and thy faithfulness reacheth unto the clouds. Thy righteousness is like the great mountains; thy judgements are a great deep: O Lord, thou preservest man and beast" (Psalm 36:5–6, KJV).

"Even the sparrow has found a home and the swallow a nest for herself, where she may have her young—a place near your altar, O Lord Almighty, my king and my God" (Psalm 84:3, NIV).

"Say among the heathen that the Lord reigneth: the world also shall be established that it shall not be moved: he shall judge the people righteously. Let the heavens rejoice, and let the earth be glad; let the sea roar and the fullness thereof. Let the field be joyful, and all that is therein: then shall all the trees of the wood rejoice. Before the Lord: for he cometh; for he cometh to judge the earth: he shall judge the world with righteousness, and the people with his truth" (Psalm 96:10–13, KJV).

"Let the sea roar, and the fullness thereof; the world, and they that dwell therein. Let the floods clap their hands: let the hills be joyful together before the Lord; for he cometh to judge the earth; with righteousness shall he judge the world, and the people with equity" (Psalm 98:7–9, KJV).

"Bless the Lord, all his works in all places of his dominion: bless the Lord, O my soul" (Psalm 103:22, KJV).

> He sendeth the springs into the valleys, which run among the hills. They give drink to every beast of the field: the wild asses quench their thirst. By them shall the fowls of the heaven have their habitation, which sing among the branches.
>
> He watereth the hills from his chambers: the earth is satisfied with the fruit of thy works. He causeth the grass to grow for the cattle, and herb for the service of man: that he may bring forth food out of the earth; and wine that maketh glad the heart of man, and oil to make his face to shine, and bread which strengthen man's heart.
>
> The trees of the Lord are full of sap; the cedars of Lebanon, which he hath planted; where the birds make their nests: as for the stork, the fir trees are her house. The high hills are a refuge for the wild goats; and the rocks for the conies. He appointed the moon for seasons: the sun knoweth his going down. Thou makest darkness, and it is night: wherein all the beasts of the forest do creep forth. The young lions roar after their prey, and seek their meat from God. The sun ariseth, they gather themselves together, and lay them down in their dens. (Psalm 104:10–22, KJV)

"He looketh on the earth, and it trembleth: he toucheth the hills, and they smoke" (Psalm 104:32, KJV).

> The Lord is good to all: and his tender mercies are over all his works. All thy works shall praise thee, O Lord; and thy saints shall bless thee. They shall speak of the glory of thy kingdom, and talk of thy power, to make known to the sons of men his mighty acts, and the glorious majesty of his kingdom, and thy dominion endureth throughout all generations. The Lord upholdeth all that fall, and raiseth up all those that be bowed down. The eyes of all wait upon thee; and thou givest them their meat in due season. Thou openest thine hand, and satisfies the desire of every living thing. The Lord is righteous in all his ways, and holy in all his works. The Lord is nigh unto all them that call upon him, to all that call upon him in truth. He will fulfill the desire of them that fear him: he also will hear their cry, and will save them. The Lord preserveth all them that love him: but all the wicked will he destroy. My mouth shall speak the praise of the Lord: and let all flesh bless his holy name for ever and ever. (Psalm 145:9–21, KJV)

"He giveth to the beast his food, and to the young raven which cry" (Psalm 147:9, KJV).

> Praise ye him, sun and moon: praise him, all ye stars of light. Praise him, ye heavens of heavens, and ye waters that be above the heavens. Let them praise the name of the Lord: for he commanded, and they were created. He hath also established them for ever and ever: he hath made a decree which shall not pass.

> Praise the Lord from the earth, ye dragons, and all deeps. Fire, and hail; snow, and vapour; stormy wind fulfilling his word:

mountains, and all hills; fruitful trees, and all cedars: Beasts, and all cattle; creeping things, and flying fowl. (Psalm 148:3–10, KJV)

"Let everything that hath breath praise the Lord. Praise ye the Lord" (Psalm 150:6, KJV).

The message is comforting, consistent, and sings like a beautiful song. Even though there are many more scriptures similar to these in the Bible, I wanted to share enough with you so you could truly see the consistency of the message. To me, it is amazing how often God shares about creation and His undying love for all He created. The Bible also conveys how animals look to God for their sustenance. The other strong message I get from these words is that God plans to make everything right in the end. There, again, is the glimmer of hope.

The story of Jonah is another example of God's care for humans and animals. Jonah was a prophet of God. God wanted him to go to Nineveh and preach repentance. Jonah didn't like the people of Nineveh and didn't want to go. After some coercion, which we will talk about in another chapter, Jonah finally did what God requested of him. The king and the people of Nineveh repented from their wrongdoing. The animals also played a role in this repentance:

> For word came unto the king of Nineveh, and he arose from his throne, and he laid his robe from him, and covered him with sackcloth, and sat in ashes. And he caused it to be proclaimed and published through Nineveh by the decree of the king and his nobles, saying, Let neither man nor beast, herd nor flock, taste anything: let them not feed, nor drink water: But let man and beast be covered with sackcloth, and cry mightily unto God: Yea, let them turn everyone from his evil way, and from the violence

that is in their hands. Who can tell if God will turn and repent, and turn away from his fierce anger, that we perish not?

And God saw their works, that they turned from their evil way; and God repented of the evil, that he had said that he would do unto them; and he did it not. (Jonah 3:6–10, KJV)

Even though Jonah finally did as God wanted him to, he wasn't happy. He didn't like the people of Nineveh. He knew God, being the loving God He is, would probably forgive them. He wasn't pleased about this. God talked to Jonah. God shared His concern not only for the people of Nineveh but also the cattle that lived in Nineveh. His concern isn't exclusively for humans but for animals as well: "But Nineveh has more than a hundred and twenty thousand people who cannot tell their right hand from their left, and many cattle as well. Should I not be concerned about that great city?" (Jonah 4:11, NIV).

Jesus talked frequently about God's care for all animals. He would use them as examples of perfect trust in God's care. How much we can learn from God's creatures!

"Look at the birds of the air; they do not sow or reap or store away in barns, and yet your heavenly Father feeds them. Are you not much more valuable than they?" (Matthew 6:26, NIV).

"Are not five sparrows sold for two pennies? Yet not one of them is forgotten by God?" (Luke 12:6, NIV).

"Consider the ravens: They do not sow or reap, they have no store room or barn; yet God feeds them, and how much more valuable you are than birds" (Luke 12:24, NIV).

St. Francis of Assisi knew that God loved all His creatures. He also knew how creation would sing praises to God. St. Francis would frequently talk with the animals and the birds. He is known for even preaching to them. It is said that one day when St. Francis was traveling with some companions, he saw many birds flying around and landing on some trees nearby. He told his companions to wait for him while he went to preach to his sisters the birds. The birds apparently congregated around him while he talked with them. The following prayer is apparently what he preached to the birds. It sings praises to God:

> My little sisters, the birds, much bounden are ye unto God, your Creator, and always in every place ought ye to praise Him, for that He hath given you liberty to fly about everywhere, and hath also given you double and triple raiment; moreover He preserved your seed in the ark of Noah, that your race might not perish out of the world; still more are ye beholden to Him for the element of the air which He hath appointed for you; beyond all this, ye sow not, neither do you reap; and God feedeth you, and giveth you the streams and fountains for your drink; the mountains and valleys for your refuge and the high trees whereon to make your nests; and because ye know not how to spin or sow, God clotheth you, you and your children; wherefore your Creator loveth you much, seeing that He hath bestowed on you so many benefits; and therefore, my little sisters, beware of the sin of ingratitude, and study always to give praises unto God.[5]

St. Francis understood God's word, and I believe he saw the big picture. We are all together in this world. We are all connected, because God

---

[5]   Francis of Assisi, "Sermon to the Birds" The History Placc. http://www.historyplace.com/speeches/saintfran.htm (accessed 23 June 2006)

made us all. I believe that is why St. Francis always referred to animals and birds as his brothers and sisters. We are all related. St. Francis felt the compassion of God reaching out to all of them.

God always points the way to a brighter future. Prior to ending this chapter, there are two last scriptures I want to share with you. The first one comes from the book of Isaiah, and the second is found in Revelation:

"And it shall come to pass, that from one new moon to another, and from one sabbath to another, shall all flesh come to worship before me, saith the Lord" (Isaiah 66:23, KJV).

"And every creature which is in heaven, and on the earth, and under the earth, and such as are in the sea, and all that are in them, heard I saying, Blessing, and honour, and glory, and power, be unto him that sitteth upon the throne, and unto the Lamb for ever and ever" (Revelation 5:13, KJV).

God's word is very clear that He cares for everything He has created. All creatures worship Him and will worship Him. He wants to hear from all of us. Let's sing praises to the Lord, for He is good!

Jonah's Story

photo taken by Suzy Mast-Lee

In September of 2001, just a few months after Noah came to us, Albert became sick. The doctor did a complete physical on him but could find nothing wrong from all the tests he ran. Still, Albert seemed to not feel well at all. One Sunday night in late September, Albert was doing very poorly. He was rushed to the emergency clinic. Again, nothing could be found that was really wrong with him. He had a bit of a temperature, so he was given an antibiotic, but that was it. The next night, Albert died. He was lying on my bed with Noah lying on the floor by him. It all seemed so sudden. Albert seemed to peacefully and quickly part from us. He didn't seem to be in pain, and I am glad we were there with him. Again, it was a dark day. Just as everything seemed to be getting better, Albert left. Looking back, I wonder if Albert felt it was okay to go home with Ashley. Albert loved Noah and knew I would be okay. I think he just missed Ashley too much and decided it was time for him to go and be with her.

I was concerned about Noah. He came to me wanting a home, and he found a friend in Albert. With Albert going to heaven, how would Noah cope? He loved Albert so much. When I returned to work a day later, I remember praying again, "Lord, if there is another cocker in need, send him my way." For some reason I decided to look at the website for the Humane Society. I had looked at it in the past, but I had never seen a cocker listed. This time the first dog I saw was a little six-month-old tricolor cocker spaniel boy. His listing date was October 1, the day Albert died. He apparently had been dumped in a park. He had what they call a cherry eye, which is when the third eyelid becomes detached. After he was picked up, he was taken to a vet to fix his eye. Of course I had to pursue it. I printed off a copy of a picture of this little guy and took it home. Then I started having dreams about him. For some reason I couldn't get him off my mind. I contacted the Humane Society to get information and had them fax an application to complete and send back. I went the following Saturday to see him.

What I found out about the adoption process was that they want you to come and see the pet, go home and think about it, and then come back a second time before the adoption process is completed. For me, it didn't happen that way. I went on that Saturday, saw this little cocker, paid the fee, obtained the needed paperwork, and went home with him that same day. Either it was meant for me to have him, or they desperately wanted him to go. I really think now it was the former, although at first I wasn't sure. He was quite the wild man.

Jonah came home with me on a Saturday, and by Sunday he had a reoccurrence of his eye problem. He had to go through another operation that week to rectify the problem. I am sure that whole ordeal didn't help with his disposition. Jonah seemed to be in constant movement. The process of Jonah and Noah bonding seemed to entail numerous fights. He didn't seem to like cuddling, didn't seem to like being held, and most of the time was a growly mess. Even though he showed a growly, tense exterior, his eyes told an entirely different story. His eyes were gentle and loving. I always have believed that the eyes are the gateway to the soul. I knew there was a gentle soul wanting to come out, but his outside seemed to be fighting hard to keep it in.

I tried numerous strategies to help bring out the sweetness. I spent time petting and holding him in hopes that he would start to feel comfortable and safe with me and enjoy the loving. Initially, he seemed to think this was torture. I was beginning to think maybe I had made a mistake. Maybe I had moved too fast in adopting him. When I really contemplated it, I knew I hadn't made a mistake. If I hadn't adopted him, he might have ended up with someone who wouldn't have had the patience it would take. He might have been abused or thrown out again or, worse yet, killed. Obviously I wasn't going to give up on this little guy.

With time, Jonah slowly made progress and got somewhat better. Noah seemed to learn how to deal with Jonah, and interactions improved. I would pray with Jonah every day for Jesus to help him and let his loving, gentle side shine through. Jonah's name was very fitting for him. Jonah from the Bible didn't want to do what God had called him to do, and he ran away. My Jonah seemed to be running away from letting others know his gentleness.

During the summer of 2002, something very bizarre happened. It happened on a summer morning. I was sitting in my family room reading a book. Noah and Jonah were lying on the floor by me. Jonah started to act very weird—weirder than normal. He started growling at something. He growled, turning around as if something was behind him. He kept doing this, turning this way and that, jumping onto a chair, and then turning quickly to look behind him, growling, and then jumping down onto the floor again. It truly looked like something was poking him in a teasing fashion, which was tormenting him. I know this sounds crazy, but that is what it looked like. He clearly did not appear happy with this and in fact looked miserable. The problem was I didn't see anything around him. Noah and I sat there watching this whole ordeal happen before our very eyes, feeling quite awful for Jonah and not knowing what to do.

That summer I had started on my journey to find out God's eternal plan for animals. I had been exploring everything I could learn about the spiritual world, which led me to readings on near-death experiences. I had found that there are many entities around us that we, as humans, may not see, such as angels and demons. Animals are more in tune with the spiritual realm. They can either see or sense these entities far better than we can.

When I was watching Jonah having this fit, if you will, it occurred to me that it seemed like some demon or spirit of some sort was harassing him by poking at him. A strong urge came over me to go over by Jonah and pray for him for God to put a protection shield around Jonah so nothing could harm him. That is what I did. I sat on the floor by Jonah and petted him while I prayed for God to put a protection shield around him and keep all evil spirits away. I prayed fervently to God, repeating my petition over and over. Now this is what was truly amazing and truly bizarre. Jonah had been so physically tense, appearing tormented. As I was sitting by him, he crawled up in my lap, laid down, and relaxed! No joke! I had never seen this little boy do that before. I started thanking and praising God for listening to me and answering my prayer. What I saw Jonah going through on that day I never saw again. Whatever was bothering him on that day no longer messed with him. In fact, Jonah seemed to change from that moment on. His gentle side, which I always had seen in his eyes, came out more and more. Jonah became more loving and affectionate. He started to enjoy cuddling and seemed much more relaxed. On that day in the summer of 2002 Jonah and I bonded in a very special way. We both experienced something miraculous while we sat on the floor praying to God.

I know this story sounds quite crazy, but I tell you the truth. It happened just as I have told it. You can try to explain it away, but I know what I saw, and I know the changes that have happened in both Jonah and me. I know God protects us when we cry out to Him. Jonah is no longer tormented by anything bothering him. He is no longer tense all the time. His beautiful, sweet nature shines through. My Jonah is no longer trying to fight or run away from his sweet nature; he embraces it! He still is very sensitive to situations and his environment, but I believe God has given him a very keen sense of things. Jonah will let me know if there is a bug in the house. His growl has a different pitch, and I know anytime I hear that growl, I better go look at what he found. Jonah also has a real connection with nature. I have seen Jonah walk underneath plants and low-branched trees in a very slow, methodical, almost trance-like manner. When I first saw him do this, I didn't know what he was doing and proceeded to watch him closely. I finally figured out that he was being petted by the plants and trees. In my life, I have never seen any animal do this. Now when I see Jonah going underneath the plants and trees, I know he just wants to feel their tender touch on his back. He truly is a very special dog!

Care for Animals

In a previous chapter, we discussed St. Francis of Assisi and his mission to preach to animals and birds. When I was researching information about St. Francis, I found numerous stories in which he saved animals and set them free from harm. I came across a prayer of his for animals. I believe it is a fitting way to begin this chapter on God's expectation for us to care for His creatures:

God Our Heavenly Father, You created the world to serve humanity's needs and to lead them to You. By our own fault we have lost the beautiful relationship which we once had with all your creation. Help us to see that by restoring our relationship with You we will also restore it with all Your creation. Give Us the grace to see all animals as gifts from You and to treat them with respect for they are Your creation. We pray for all animals who are suffering as a result of our neglect. May the order You originally established be once again restored to the whole world through the intercession of the Glorious Virgin Mary, the prayers of Saint Francis and the merits of Your Son,

Our Lord Jesus Christ who lives and reigns with You now and forever. Amen.[6]

As we discussed earlier, God made all things beautiful and perfect in the Garden of Eden. God placed man to have dominion over His creation. Adam and Eve were made to be caretakers of God's garden and all of His creatures. It is important to remember that God made all living creatures (humans included) to be vegetarian. It wasn't until after Noah and the ark that this changed. God's plan was for a peaceful and harmonious coexistence. There was no death, no torture, and no pain of any sort. All humans and creatures lived together as one big, happy family with God as their Father. Due to humans' disobedience and sin, everything changed and became cursed. It is because of humans' sin that all creation changed and consequently has suffered. Man's nature changed and became more and more evil. Due to man's failure to live up to the godly standard of his appointed position to care for all creation as God designed him to do, all creation was altered and radically changed from its original state. It is because of this that the nature of creatures changed. Some of the animals, birds, and fish that were once peaceful and vegetarian changed, becoming savage flesh eaters. Other animals, birds, and fish became their prey. John Wesley, founder of the Methodist Church, speaks of this in his sermon "The General Deliverance." Human's behavior changed, which had a direct impact on all creatures. Humans' original nature changed, and thus so did the nature of all creatures. It makes me wonder whether, if humans changed their vile ways, becoming more as God intended, would the creatures also change back to something closer to their original behavior?

---

[6]   Francis of Assisi. "Prayer for Animals." MyCatholicSource.com. http://www.mycatholicsource.com/mcs/pc/saint_francis_section_prayers.htm (accessed 7 April 2014)

I do believe it is possible. If man became a better caretaker instead of a destroyer, wouldn't all creation follow the good example set before it?

"For every kind of beasts, and of birds, and of serpents, and of things in the sea, is tamed, and hath been tamed of mankind: But the tongue can no man tame; it is an unruly evil, full of deadly poison" (James 3:7–8, KJV).

"But the wisdom that is from above is first pure, then peaceable, gentle, and easy to be intreated, full of mercy and good fruits, without partiality, and without hypocrisy. And the fruit of righteousness is sown in peace of them that make peace" (James 3:17–18, KJV).

"Therefore to him that knoweth to do good, and doeth it not, to him it is sin" (James 4:17, KJV).

James spared no words when discussing the evil of man and what God has called all of us to do. His words strike to the truth of the matter. Even though man has fallen away from God's original plan, He still reaches out to all of us through His word to draw us back to His way and His design. There are a multitude of scriptures that entreat us to care for all of God's creatures in a peaceable, gentle manner. I am quite astounded at the number of them. Let me share some of them with you.

God intertwines His message in the different stories of the Bible. Stories are a great teaching tool. They give us a picture to look at and learn from, something we can hold on to and remember. Remember the story of Noah and the ark? I won't repeat the scriptures here, because we covered them in detail in a previous chapter. God gave us many lessons within that story. He revealed His care for and desire to save a remnant of all animal and bird species. He instructed Noah to care for all of them while on the ark. Let's move on and look at the story of

Abraham. Abraham is described as a friend of God. God gave Abraham a promise that all nations would be blessed through him and his seed. He and Sarah had a son, Isaac, when they were both extremely old. The part I want to focus on is a bit later in the story. Sarah had died by this time, and Isaac had grown into manhood. Abraham was concerned about finding a wife for his son. Abraham sent his eldest servant to go to his home country to find a wife for Isaac. The servant did as Abraham requested. This was an important task. The servant was sent to find the right mate for Abraham's son, the one whom God's promise to Abraham would be passed through. The servant took ten camels with him. Once he got to his destination, he and his camels knelt down outside the city by a well. He prayed for God to bring the right woman to him for Isaac to marry:

> And he said, O Lord God of my master Abraham, I pray thee, send me good speed this day, and shew kindness unto my master Abraham. Behold, I stand here by the well of water, and the daughters of the men of the city come out to draw water: And let it come to pass, that the damsel to whom I shall say, Let down thy pitcher, I pray thee, that I may drink; and she shall say, Drink, and *I will give thy camels drink also:* let the same be she that thou hast appointed for thy servant Isaac; and thereby shall I know that thou hast shewed kindness unto my master. (Genesis 24:12–14, KJV, emphasis added)

Now you may wonder why Abraham's servant prayed a prayer like that. God is definitely trying to give us a clear message here. To me, I can see the reasoning for it. A person who cares for animals and their needs exemplifies good character—a person who can look beyond him or herself and see the needs of others, especially the needs of one of God's lesser creatures. If a person disregards the needs of animals, it conveys that he or she really doesn't care for the things of God. Remember, God made everybody and everything and dearly loves them all. As the story continues, Rebekah came out to the well to fill her pitcher: "And the servant ran to meet her, and said, Let me, I pray thee, drink a little water of thy pitcher. And she said, Drink, my lord: and she hasted, and let down her pitcher upon her hand, and gave him drink,. And when she had done giving him drink, she said, *I will draw water for thy camels also, until they have done drinking.* And she hasted, and emptied her pitcher into the trough, and ran again unto the well to draw water, *and drew for all his camels*" (Genesis 24:17–20, KJV, emphasis added).

This was a sign from God, and it spoke of Rebekah's character and integrity. Here was a woman who cared for the things of God. She later offered boarding for Abraham's servant and the camels: "She said moreover unto him, *We have both straw and provender enough, and room to lodge in*" (Genesis 24:25, KJV, emphasis added).

Not only did she give water to the camels but she offered food and lodging. They were weary from their journey. Rebekah must have seen this in their tired disposition. She offered help. The next verse states, "And the man bowed down his head, and worshipped the Lord" (Genesis 24:26). His prayers had been answered. Rebekah ran back to her home to let her brother Laban know. Laban came out to greet the man and his camels. "And he said, Come in, thou blessed of the Lord; wherefore stands thou without? for I have prepared the house, *and he ungirded his camels, and gave straw and provender for the camels,* and water to wash his feet, and the men's feet that were with him" (Genesis 24:31–32, KJV, emphasis added).

This isn't put in scripture to make for a better story; there are important messages here that we need to learn from. Caring for animals (God's creatures) is one of God's expectations of us. Making sure they have water, food, and shelter is important. It is part of our responsibility to them and to God. God wants us to care for each other, including all of His creatures.

Later in Genesis we meet Jacob, Isaac and Rebekah's son. Even though Jacob was a trickster, he knew the value of caring for his animals: "Jacob, however, went to Succoth, where he built a place for himself and *made shelters for his livestock*. That is why the place is called Succoth" (Genesis 33:17, NIV, emphasis added).

Jacob didn't only build a place for himself and disregard his livestock; he made a shelter for his animals also. I don't think this is included in the Bible for no reason. There is a reason behind everything God does. When you have animals under your charge—under your dominion, if you will—you have responsibility for caring for them and their needs. Shelter, food, and water are the basic essentials for life. God includes these expectations in His word, using stories to provide examples. Take note at the pattern and repeated message in the scriptures.

Another illustration of caring for animals is found in the story of Joseph. Joseph's brothers journeyed down to Egypt to obtain food due to a great famine in the land. I won't go into the entire story, but there is a verse that we need to look at: "the steward took the men into Joseph's house, gave them water to wash their feet and *provided fodder for their donkeys*" (Genesis 43:24, NIV, emphasis added).

Another example is in the book of Judges: "So he took him into his house and *fed his donkeys*. After they had washed their feet, they had something to eat and drink" (Judges 19:21, NIV, emphasis added).

Again, this verse shows the need to care for others and also their animals. Do you see the repetition going on? The same message is repeated over and over.

Moses obtained the laws from God for the Israelites to follow. When Moses gave instruction to the Israelites for the Sabbath day, the instruction included more than just for the people of Israel. Please take notice.

"Remember the Sabbath day, to keep it holy. Six days shalt thou labour, and do all thy work: But the seventh day is the Sabbath of the Lord thy God: in it thou shalt not do any work, thou, nor thy son, nor thy daughter, thy manservant, nor thy maidservant, *nor thy cattle,* nor thy stranger that is within thy gates: For in six days the Lord made heaven and earth, the sea, and all that in them is, and rested the seventh day: wherefore the Lord blessed the Sabbath day, and hallowed it" (Exodus 20:8–11, KJV, emphasis added).

Why would God include the animals if they aren't important to Him? He knew they also needed a day of rest. This is repeated in Deuteronomy: "but the seventh day is a Sabbath to the Lord your God. On it you shall not do any work, neither you, nor your son or daughter, nor your manservant or maidservant, *nor your ox, your donkey or any of your animals,* nor the alien within your gates, so that your manservant and maidservant may rest, as you do" (Deuteronomy 5:14, NIV, emphasis added).

In Leviticus God instructs Moses on the seventh year being a year of Sabbath:

> For six years sow your fields, and for six years prune your vineyards and gather their crops. But in the seventh year the land is to have a Sabbath of rest, a Sabbath to the Lord. So not sow your fields or prune your vineyards. Do not reap what grows of itself or harvest the grapes of your untended vines. The land is to have a year of rest. Whatever the land yields during the Sabbath year will be food for you—for yourself; your hired worker and temporary

resident who live among you, *as well as for your livestock and the wild animals in your land.* Whatever the land produces may be eaten. (Leviticus 25:3–7, NIV, emphasis added)

God would provide for all, including the livestock and the wild animals in their land. The message is very clear. God provides for all creatures, and He expects us to do the same. Again I say God would not have put it in His word if this were not important to Him.

Next I would like to share scriptures I found on how we should treat others and animals. I found them quite interesting, and I hope you do too.

"If you come across your enemy's donkey wandering off, be sure to take it back to him. If you see the donkey of someone who hates you fallen down under its load, do not leave it there; be sure you help him with it" (Exodus 23:4–5, NIV).

"Thou shalt not see thy brother's ox or his sheep go astray, and hide thyself from them: thou shalt in any case bring them again unto thy brother. And if thy brother be not nigh unto thee, or if thou know him not, then thou shalt bring it unto thine own house, and it shall be with thee until thy brother seek after it, and thou shalt restore it to him again" (Deuteronomy 22:1–2, KJV).

"If you see your brother's donkey or his ox fallen on the road, do not ignore it. Help him get it to its feet" (Deuteronomy 22:4, NIV).

God is calling all of us to be compassionate; to help each other out no matter what our disagreements may be; and to think of those animals that have fallen, are having trouble of some kind, or are lost. No matter what may be our hard feelings toward each other, the innocent animals didn't do anything wrong and don't deserve to be treated unkindly.

"If you come across a bird's nest beside the road, either in a tree or on the ground, and the mother is sitting on the young or on eggs, do not take the mother with the young. You may take the young, but be sure to let the mother go, so that it may go well with you and you may have a long life" (Deuteronomy 22:6–7, NIV).

I wanted to be sure that I was interpreting these passages correctly. I consulted *The Interpreter's Bible*[7] for their interpretation. *The Interpreter's Bible* describes these passages as "The Law of Kindness." Here is their explanation of the passages: "This is not really a legal provision, but it illustrates what will be everyone's daily conduct when the true spirit of Yahweh is at work in his heart. Courtesy and tender consideration of others will extend even to the birds in their nests."[8]

Deuteronomy 24:4 says, "Do not muzzle an ox while it is treading out the grain" (NIV). I checked the *The Interpreter's Bible* on this scripture as well. It says, "This law, like the preceding, occurs only in Deuteronomy, and seems to be motivated by the principle of love and kindness which should be shown to all God's creatures."[9]

Okay, so I'm not off track with how I understand the scriptures. I found it interesting and encouraging that others have seen this same message that God is desperately trying to communicate. It may seem like I am including too many scriptures and belaboring the point. The problem is that we have been missing the point for too long. It is easier not to look

---

[7]   H. Shires, and P. Parker "The Book of Deuteronomy" in *The Interpreter's Bible, Vol. II,* ed. W.R. Bowie, et al. (Nashville: Abingdon-Cokesbury Press, 1953), 463
[8]   Ibid., 463
[9]   Ibid., 479

outside our comfort zone. We think that as long as we don't see it, we don't have to do anything about it. I believe many people like to live with blinders on. It makes life easier and less painful. But is that truly what God wants? Are we, as His people, supposed to set the standard instead of succumbing to the world's standard? We need to go to His word for answers and direction. We need to take responsibility for our actions and make a change to live more according to God's will, not our own.

In Proverbs the same message is being sent. We are still seeing repetition and consistency throughout the Bible. I will share this verse from the Kings James Version and also from the New International Version. In the King James Version, Proverbs 12:10 reads, "A righteous man regardeth the life of his beast: but the tender mercies of the wicked are cruel." The New International Version translates the same passage this way: "A righteous man cares for the needs of his animal, but the kindest acts of the wicked are cruel."

I don't believe I can make it any clearer than that. Someone would have to be very spiritually blind not to see God's expectations of us and how we are all responsible to do our part to care for God's creatures.

Jesus spoke on these matters. Three of the scriptures I will be sharing pertain to working on the Sabbath day. Jesus frequently used analogies for teaching purposes. Take notice of what He chooses for the analogies. It speaks volumes about His love and care for all of His creatures.

"He said to them, 'If any of you has a sheep and it falls into a pit on the Sabbath, will you not take hold of it and lift it out?'" (Matthew 12:11, NIV).

"The Lord answered him, 'You hypocrites! Doesn't each of you on the Sabbath untie his ox or donkey from the stall and lead it out to give it water?'" (Luke 13:15, NIV).

"And answered them, saying Which of you shall have an ass or an ox fallen into a pit, and will not straightway pull him out on the sabbath day?" (Luke 14:5, KJV).

And then I have one more: "How think ye? If a man have an hundred sheep, and one of them be gone astray, doth he not leave the ninety and nine, and goeth into the mountains, and seeketh that which is gone astray? And if so be that he find it, verily I say unto you, he rejoiceth more of that sheep, than the ninety and nine which went not astray. Even so it is not the will of your Father which in heaven, that one of these little ones should perish" (Matthew 18:12–14, KJV).

Jesus may be describing the importance of each one of us in God's eyes, but it would be negligent on our part to overlook the true importance of the total message. All God's creatures are important, not just humans. If we truly love God and want to do His will, we cannot ignore His message. We cannot just pick and choose what we will do for God. I keep going back to the scripture that God planted in my heart early on in my journey. Jesus was sitting on the Mount of Olives and talking with His disciples, teaching them and giving them guidance. Jesus was sharing about things to come and the need to be diligent to His instructions. Here is what he said:

> Then shall the King say unto them on his right hand, Come, ye blessed of my Father, inherit the kingdom prepared for you from the foundation of the world: For I was an hungered, and ye gave me meat: I was thirsty, and ye gave me drink: I was a stranger, and ye took me in: Naked, and ye clothed me: I was sick, and ye visited me: I was in prison, and ye came unto me.

Then shall the righteous answer him saying, Lord, when saw we thee an hungered, and fed thee? or thirsty, and gave thee drink? When saw we thee a stranger, and took thee in? or naked, and clothed thee? Or when saw we thee sick, or in prison, and came unto thee?

And the King shall answer and say unto them, Verily I say unto you, Inasmuch as ye have done it unto one of the least of these my brethren, ye have done it unto me. Then shall he say also unto them on the left hand, Depart from me, ye cursed, into everlasting fire, prepared for the devil and his angels: For I was an hungered, and ye gave me no meat: I was thirsty, and ye gave me no drink: I was a stranger, and ye took me not in: naked, and ye clothed me not: sick, and in prison, and ye visited me not.

Then shall they also answer him, saying, Lord, when saw we thee an hungered, or athirst, or a stranger, or naked, or sick, or in prison, and did not minister unto thee?

Then shall he answer them, saying, Verily I say unto you, Inasmuch as ye did it not to one of the least of these, ye did it not to me.

And these shall go away into everlasting punishment: but the righteous into life eternal. (Matthew 25:34–46, KJV)

Take a look at our world today. Woodland areas are being destroyed to make way for new housing subdivisions. Woods and country meadows for animals to live in are cleared away to make way for what we call progress. Does anybody care what happens to the creatures and birds that once made their homes in the trees and the brush? They have been pushed out and left homeless. We then complain about too many deer running out in traffic, causing wrecks. Whose fault is it really? Who is really being mistreated and losing their precious lives, and at whose hands? And then there are animals being used to test products that we use. They are treated horribly and usually destroyed when humans are done with them, or they lead incredibly horrid lives. Is that really what they were put on this earth for—to be used and destroyed as humans see fit? Are we really doing justice and being good stewards of what God has given us dominion over? Or are we grossly destroying God's creation? I am sure God is weeping over the destruction and decay that we have brought to His glorious creation. We all will be held responsible for all our actions and the decisions we make. I take the word seriously. I believe Jesus is trying desperately to show us the way and how we need to treat each other and all of His creatures. It is important to me to serve the least of these.

In closing this chapter, I want to share a dream that Pope John Paul II had prior to becoming the Pope. I found the dream very moving. I hope you will be moved as well. I am far from being alone on my concern regarding how we treat others and God's creatures. The dream is told in its entirety in the book *God's Broker: The Life of John Paul II* by Antoni Gronowicz. He had the dream while he was visiting Canada. The dream had taken place during the winter months in New York City following a severe snow storm. The entire city was covered with mounds of snow. In his dream, Pope John Paul II was walking along the streets of an upscale part of NYC. There were nice apartment buildings lining the road. As he walked along he noticed a mother cat and her kittens emerge from the snow seeking shelter from the bitter cold.

> On top of the snow, I noticed a brown cat emerge from a side street and walk on the snow. I looked closer, and to my surprise, saw that this big cat was being followed by six small

brown-and-white kittens, all of them following the big cat in a perfect line. The mother cat looked back from time to time to see if her babies were there, but her main concern was to reach the entrance door. I presume she was trying to find warmth for herself and her children, but as soon as she reached the door, a man in a well-pressed uniform jumped at her with a broom and chased them away. I followed this procession and prepared to deliver a speech to the doorman. I opened my mouth and tried to complain, "Where is your proverbial American generosity? Where is your American good heart and fair play? Let them in. Let them in!" I tried to speak, but the words would not come out.[10]

He continued to follow after the little cat family. The momma cat tried to seek refuge at a couple of different churches but the churches turned her and her babies away. Pope John Paul II was furious with the lack of care, empathy, and hospitality that was given to the poor momma cat and her kittens. He was also frustrated that he couldn't seem to say anything or speak up for them in their time of need. He continued to follow the momma cat and her kittens as they traveled on down the road. The fancy buildings slowly went away as they were entering a less desirable and less cared for part of the city.

As they walked and the buildings grew shabbier and dirty, a door opened, not by a doorman but by an old wrinkled woman in a cotton dress. She shouted, "Oh mama mia," and when she opened her mouth I saw she had no teeth.

---

10 Antoni Gronowicz, *God's Broker: The Life of John Paul II,* (New York: Richardson & Snider, 1984) 311-314

She gently ushered the mother cat and kittens inside, who jumped happily about because the warmth of the house embraced them."[11]

When I read this dream, I thought of the story of the widow giving two mites into the treasury. Two mites only equaled about four cents. Jesus said in Mark 12:43-44, "Verily I say unto you, That this poor widow hath cast more in, than all they which have cast into the treasury: For all they did cast in of their abundance; but she of her want did cast in all that she had, even all her living" (KJV). The ones that could have given much, gave nothing. The woman who had little to give, gave the cat family a home and shelter from the storm.

The dream of Pope John Paul II apparently had a deep effect on him—enough of an impact that he felt compelled to share it. It is evident that he believed his dream had a deep meaning. God tries desperately to speak out to each one of us. He wants us to walk in His ways. I know He has given us His word through the Bible. I also believe He speaks to us in many ways and in many forms. Dreams can be one of the mechanisms He uses to reach our souls about His truth. The next story I am going to share with you is an example of how God has reached me through dreams. Coincidentally, it also is about cats.

---

[11]   Ibid., 311-314

Cat Story

Many years ago, my mom and I had been enjoying a girl's day out together. We had gone shopping and out to lunch, and we were enjoying our time together—quality time. We were on our way back to her home when we saw a black, gray, and white tiger cat in the middle of the highway. It had been run over on its hind quarters and couldn't move out of the road. It was still alive. My mom told me to pull over. She couldn't allow this poor, helpless cat to stay in the middle of the road waiting for some uncaring person to finish the job of killing him. She ran out in the road, picked up the cat and took it over to the side of the road in the ditch. I got a blanket out of the back of my car to put it around the cat. A truck driver stopped to see if we needed help. When he found out it was a cat that had been run over, he responded in disgust, "A cat!" He turned around and left. My mom ordered, "We've got to get him to a vet!" After getting my mom and the cat settled in the car, I hurried to the driver's side, and we took off.

At that time, I had only recently moved out to the country. My folks had lived out there for several years. I didn't know where the closest vet was. My mom was aware of one not too far away. I was going as fast as I could safely go. I also need to say that I was terrified. I didn't always do well with crisis situations like this. I wanted to help out animals in need, but to be quite honest, I would freak out. Feelings of helplessness would envelop me and inhibit my actions. I am not proud to say that about myself. My mom was the exact opposite. She would see a need and go into action. There was no hesitation with her.

We finally made it to the vet. It was closed due to the vet being on vacation. What now? We headed toward Harrisonville, the next closest town. We found another vet office. The doctor was out making a house call and wouldn't be back until later. The cat was moaning, obviously in immense pain. Mom said to head back toward Cleveland and head over to Louisburg. She knew there was a vet on the main road through town. I zoomed off in that direction. Mom kept saying that if we could save this cat, it would be hers. She knew she would keep it. Gordon, her husband (my pop), wouldn't be able to say anything about it. She continued to stroke the cat, trying to comfort him as much as she could. We finally made it to the Louisburg vet. We got the cat in the office, and they immediately took the poor cat back to a room. The doctor came out shortly and said that the little boy just passed away. When it was run over, there was extensive internal damage. He was bleeding internally. Mom and I both wept. She wouldn't leave him there. She was going to take this little cat home and give him a proper burial. We rapped him up in the blanket and took him home. Mom told Gordon about what happened and that she needed him to dig a grave. She told him where she wanted it to be. It was a beautiful, shady spot among the trees. He did exactly what she asked, and we had a funeral for the cat. Even though we didn't know the cat long, he changed us. I saw a side of my mom that was beautiful. She faced a situation and did what was right even if it would cause inconvenience and pain. She wouldn't let that cat die alone. What courage that woman had; what compassion she possessed. She is my hero, and she was the cat's angel.

Even though my mom had a heart of gold, her natural heart had become weak and sick. In May of 2004 she went in the hospital for open-heart surgery. A week later, on June 3, she died. The world lost an amazing, compassionate lady. Heaven won a beautiful soul. It was a very dark time in my life when she left this world. My mom was my best friend. I learned so much from that woman. I am who I am because of her.

It was around the time that my mom died that I noticed a momma cat and her kittens staying in an old, dilapidated shed I had. The kittens were already several weeks old when I noticed them. I watched them play from a distance. They were pretty wild and wouldn't let anyone get too close. One day they left, and I never saw them again. I guess I ought to let you know that I am not a huge fan of cats. I am more a dog person. Well, I love all animals, and don't get me wrong—I don't want anything bad to happen to cats; I just don't care to live with one. I guess my feeling toward cats goes back to my childhood. My two sisters (who were quite a bit older than me) were always cat people. They didn't like dogs. I never had close relationships with my sisters growing up. I think this was partly because I was so much younger. They always tried to take on more of a parental role than the sisterly role. Because this story isn't so much about my relationship with my sisters as it is about cats, let me press forward and not dwell on the details. Anyway, for whatever reason, I think I always associated cats with my sisters, and I wanted to keep both at a respectable distance.

In September, I heard some faint sounds coming from that old shed. When I opened up the door I found three little bitty baby kittens. They were smaller than tennis balls. They were black, gray, and white tiger cats. One of them had longer hair than the other two. The little kittens were on top of a big mound of insulation. To get an accurate picture of this sight, I need to tell you something about my husband. You know the old saying "Out of sight, out of mind"? I think this was his motto. He had been using this old, dilapidated shed as a junk storage container. He had stuffed it with old junk and mounds of unused insulation. It truly was a total wreck. The little kittens were on top of the insulation. One had fallen back between the insulation mounds and the other junk that occupied this dinky shed. Needless to say, we had to remove the insulation and some of the junk to make a safer place for these kittens. After it was emptied, I found a box and placed an old blanket in it. I put the kittens in the box and prayed that the momma cat would come back to take care of them. Momma Kitty did return to care for her kittens. She was a wild cat and would not let us get too close. When Momma Kitty was not around, the little kittens would let us pick them up. They were too young to be wild and were no more than a week or so old.

I made sure they had fresh water and provided food for them. At first I gave them dog food, because that was all we had. Later I started buying kitty food for them. I checked on the kittens daily, replenishing their food and water. If Momma Kitty was in the shed, she would growl ferociously. The more we came around and provided for their needs, the friendlier Momma Kitty became. She would growl initially, but after realizing it was only us, she would purr and rub up against our legs. She began letting us even pet her. The kittens would always want to play and never showed any fear. Even though I am not a cat person, they sure were cute.

I remember having a dream about the cats. All the kittens were in our house. They were all making themselves at home. Momma Kitty was in the house, but she seemed very nervous and agitated. I remember thinking that I needed to get her back into the shed; she wasn't comfortable with the surroundings of the house and having people around. I got a blanket and wrapped her up so I could get her back outside. I also remember thinking I had to bring the kittens out to her. It was kind of a weird dream, but it was only a dream.

The kittens were getting a little bit bigger and started to venture outside of the shed. I guess it was around the beginning of November. I came home from work one evening, and all the cats were gone. It was kind of sad. I missed them. The next morning they were still gone. They had been gone for about a week or so when I had another dream about the cats. I dreamed that they all had come back. I told my husband about my dream in the morning. I remember him saying, "Wouldn't it be weird if it came true?" I laughed at this. He went outside to start on the morning chores. When he came back in the house he said, "Dwila, you are weird." I responded with "What?" He then told me that the cats were all back—every one of them. Of course we were happy to see them, but I also was a bit amazed about my dream. I mean, I just had the dream that the cats had returned and *bam*—they were back!

A couple of weeks went by. The cats stayed around home. They would leave for part of the day and then return. Then they left and didn't come back. A couple of weeks or more went by and they were still gone. I really thought that this time they were gone for good. Then I had another dream. I dreamed about the cats, and that they all returned again. I got up in the morning, recalling my dream, and wondered if it would come true again. Then I thought, *No, that's impossible.* I got ready for work and woke my husband up before I left. I have an hour drive to work, so I leave before the sun even comes up. I told him about my dream. He said if this one came true, something was very bizarre about my dreams. I grabbed my things, kissed him good-bye, and left out the back door.

As I was walking toward the driveway I saw the old, dilapidated shed. Then I saw a pair of glowing eyes and then another pair of glowing eyes. The cats were back! Of course I had to turn around and go back inside to relay this information. He was speechless. I asked him to make sure they had food and water. Two dreams about the cats, and both dreams came true immediately after I had them. This was too bizarre for me. I also knew there was something going on beyond my comprehension. God was doing something. I didn't quite understand what, but I knew He had to be up to something with all this.

It was about a week before Christmas. We had been gone all day enjoying festivities of the season. Upon returning home, we were faced with a horrible sight. All the cats were gone except for Momma Kitty, who was severely injured. Something had ripped her open along her side. She was howling in terrible pain. My husband rushed her to the animal emergency room. He called after Momma Kitty had been seen. They couldn't save her. Whatever had gotten her had ripped her up bad inside. All her organs were messed up and moved around. They recommended that we have her put to sleep to put her out of her misery. He said she was purring in his arms when she went to sleep.

After the call, I went outside to pray and cry. I looked out to the old dilapidated shed. I saw four glowing eyes. Two of the kittens had returned. What was I to do? They don't know it yet, but their momma had just died. She wouldn't be back to take care of them. I knew what it was like to lose a momma. Oh, gosh, I wished I could talk with my mom to see what to do. I so missed her right then. I did what I thought was the right thing to do. I brought the two kittens inside. I looked around for the third one but couldn't find her.

We never saw Gracie, the other kitten, again. I don't know if she was with Momma Kitty when she was attacked. I like to hope that someone picked her up and took her in. She was a beautiful little kitty. Chloe and Sam took to the home life. The initial challenge was to see if our dogs would take to the kittens. It took a little time, but they all seemed to get along famously. Noah took over the job of being their momma. He would mother them, licking them all over. The kittens would close their eyes and let him do whatever to them. They would even sleep together side by side.

I took the cats to the vet to get their shots and to have them spayed and neutered. I felt it was our responsibility to at least take care of this, and then the plan was to find good homes for them with a family that would take care of them and love them the way they needed to be loved. We also thought it was important to keep them together. They had already lost a mom and a sister. All they had was each other, and we didn't want to take that away from them.

Well, we were not making any progress with finding them homes. Our house was being taken over by all of our critters; and let us not forget that I am not too fond of cats, so I wasn't too thrilled with the idea of keeping them permanently. Oh, and did I mention that I was allergic to cats? My eyes would get puffy, and I would start breaking out in a rash. I don't know if my allergy was somehow related to my feelings about cats and my sisters. I don't remember being allergic when I was little, but who knows? And then I remembered the dreams. I have never had dreams that came true immediately before. Well, there was a time when I was a little kid and my grandmother, who had multiple sclerosis, was staying with us. This was the grandmother that I was very close to. She was wheelchair bound. We put a bed up in our living room. I slept on the couch in the same room with her. I remember having a dream—well, it was more of a talking dream in which someone was talking to me about my grandmother. I was told that the lock on her wheelchair was not locked and that when she tried to get in it from bed, it would move and she would fall on the floor. I was questioned about what I would do. I decided I would call my mom at work. I was told that was a good plan. I then woke up to a thud and then giggling. My grandmother was trying to get in her wheelchair. The lock on the chair was not in place, and the chair moved. My grandmother fell on the floor. She was okay, even giggling about what had happened, but I wasn't big enough to get her into her chair. Without hesitation, I called my mom at work, and she came home to help. That is the only other dream I can remember that I had and it came true immediately. That dream helped me deal with a situation in a calm way, especially since I was the only one at home with my grandmother at the time. I knew that the dreams about the cats meant something. I had two dreams that the cats came back after being away, and the morning after each dream, they were back. Those dreams were not just a coincidence; God was telling me something.

The cats were slowly getting under my skin. My allergies were slowly subsiding. Was I just getting used to them, or was my allergy going away? I don't really know. God was working with me on past issues. One thing He told me was that even though my sisters were not nice to me growing up, these cats didn't do anything wrong; they were not to blame for my sisters' past actions. It is hard for me to explain what exactly happened to me. All I know is that I was healing, learning to forgive and letting go of the past. Was this the reason God sent these cats to me? I sometimes wonder if my mom had a part in bringing the cats. The cat we couldn't save that was run over on the highway came back to my mind. My mom planned to keep the cat if he lived. He didn't, but she was with him at the end, and he didn't die alone. I know she is with that cat now in heaven. These cats look like that cat—same coloring and everything. I guess I will never know for sure if my mom played a part in all of this or not. I will find out someday when I join her in heaven. I do know God was involved in all of it. He has used these two kittens to help heal me from past pain. Momma Kitty knows we are taking care of her babies. She trusted us, and I couldn't let her down. When faced with a situation, it is important to do what is right even if it may cause inconvenience and pain. That's what I learned from my momma.

Symbolism, a Talking Donkey, and Other Hidden Messages

This chapter is about a dance that God does with us, animals, and all creation. He tries desperately to show us how we are all interconnected and interrelated. We are all intertwined, humans and creatures, all interwoven and linked together. Without one or the other, things would be out of balance. It takes all of creation to keep the balance. God is whole, and His design is whole and perfect. To show the interconnectedness, God uses animals as active participants in the messages and stories of the Bible. God also uses animals as an illustration to drive home the meaning of an important lesson. I also see how God interweaves the connection through symbolism and what could be thought of as hidden messages. It is possible that many people have overlooked the importance of some of the true treasures of God's word because they simply weren't looking for them. I also know there are countless ones who have found exactly what I have. Always continue to search God's word for yourself. It is always amazing to me the wealth of wisdom that can be found in the Bible when you open your eyes, your heart, and your mind to it.

In the Garden of Eden, Satan used the serpent to speak the words of distortion and lies in order to tempt Adam and Eve. In the story of Noah and the ark, God intermingles His plan to save a remnant of animals and humans. He shares the importance of humans' position to care for all God's creatures. He makes a covenant not only with humans but also with all creatures He has made. In the book of Jonah, God uses a big fish to swallow up Jonah. Jonah was a prophet that didn't really want to do what God had asked him to do. God used the big fish to get his attention. "Now the Lord had prepared a great fish to swallow up Jonah. And Jonah was in the belly of the fish three days and three nights" (Jonah 1:17, KJV).

The great fish, which many think was a whale, although it doesn't say, obeyed God and did what he was told. The great fish swallowed up Jonah, and there he was for three days and three nights. Jonah finally prayed to God, realizing where he had gone wrong, and agreed to do what he was called to do: "But I will sacrifice unto thee with the voice of thanksgiving; I will pay that that I have vowed. Salvation is of the Lord" (Jonah 2:9, KJV). The Lord heard Jonah's prayer and spoke to the great fish. "And the Lord spake unto the fish, and it vomited out Jonah upon the dry land" (Jonah 2:10, KJV). The fish did exactly what God told him to do. It wasn't like the fish would go against God and say, "Oh, I think I would rather not, Lord." Animals are obedient and totally trust God.

Let us now look at the story of Balaam and his donkey:

> And God came unto Balaam at night, and said unto him, If the men come to call thee; rise up, and go with them; but yet the word which I shall say unto thee, that shall thou do. And Balaam rose up in the morning, and saddled his ass, and went with the princes of Moab. And God's anger was kindled because

he went: and the angel of the Lord stood in the way for an adversary against him. Now he was riding upon his ass, and his two servants were with him. And the ass saw the angel of the Lord standing in the way, and his sword drawn in his hand: and the ass turned aside out of the way, and went into the field: and Balaam smote the ass, to turn her into the way. But the angel of the Lord stood in a path of the vineyards, a wall being on this side, and a wall on that side. And when the ass saw the angel of the Lord, she thrust herself unto the wall, and crushed Balaam's foot against the wall: and he smote her again. And the angel of the Lord went further, and stood in a narrow place, where was no way to turn either to the right hand or to the left. And when the ass saw the angel of the Lord, she fell down under Balaam: and Balaam's anger was kindled, and he smote the ass with a staff. And the Lord opened the mouth of the ass, and she said unto Balaam, What have I done unto thee, that thou hast smitten me these three times? And Balaam said unto the ass, Because thou hast mocked me: I would there were a sword in mine hand, for now would I kill thee. And the ass said unto Balaam, Am not I thine ass, upon which thou hast ridden ever since I was thine unto this day? Was I ever wont to do so unto thee? And he said, Nay. Then the Lord opened the eyes of Balaam, and he saw the angel of the Lord standing in the way, and his sword drawn in his hand: and he bowed down his head, and fell flat on his face. And the angel of the Lord said unto him, Wherefore hast thou smitten thine ass these three times? Behold, I went out to withstand thee, because thy way is perverse before me: And the ass saw me, and turned from me these three times: unless she had turned from me, surely now also I had slain thee, and saved her alive. (Numbers 22:20–33, KJV)

There are many messages here for us to learn from. The donkey's eyes were already open to seeing spiritual things. The angel of the Lord had to open Balaam's eyes before he could truly see. The donkey, being a loyal beast, was trying only to protect her master. Balaam responded in a very cruel manner toward his donkey. The Lord opened the donkey's mouth so she could speak to Balaam in a language and a voice that he could understand. When Balaam could see the Lord before him, he finally bowed down. The Lord responded to Balaam and scolded him for how he treated his donkey and pointed out his wicked ways. One more point here not to miss: the Lord told Balaam if it wasn't for his donkey keeping him from crossing the Lord's path, He would have killed Balaam and spared his donkey. The donkey was innocent and a loyal companion. The donkey saved Balaam's life. Balaam, on the other hand, not only had wickedness in his heart but also treated his donkey in a wicked fashion. These are important lessons for us all to take to heart.

God uses animals, even insects, to teach us about wisdom and trust. In the book of Proverbs, the ant is used to teach us wisdom: "Go to the ant, sluggard; consider her ways, and be wise: which having no guide, overseer, or ruler, provideth her meat in the summer, and gathereth her food in the harvest" (Proverbs 6:6–8, KJV).

Jesus used birds to teach us about trusting God: "Consider the ravens: for they neither sow nor reap; which neither have a storehouse nor barn; and God feedeth them: how much more are ye better than the fowls?" (Luke 12:24, KJV). "Behold the fowls of the air: for they sow not, neither do they reap, nor gather into barns; yet your heavenly Father feedeth them. Are ye not much better than they?" (Matthew 6:26, KJV).

In the book of Psalms, there are countless scriptures showing how God cares for all His creatures. I've talked about these in a previous chapter, but what is so important for us to take notice of is the continual message of God's overwhelming love and care for all of His creation. All creatures rely on God to take care of them and their needs for their survival. They totally trust God. How often do we, as humans, fail to trust God to care for us?

In 1 Kings chapter 17 is the story of the prophet Elijah informing King Ahab of his prophesy of a great drought to come to the land. God told Elijah to go and stay by the brook Cherith. There he would be able to drink of the brook. God had ravens bring food to Elijah both day and night. Isn't it fascinating how God uses His creatures to work out His plan?

"And the word of the Lord came unto him, saying, Get thee hence, and turn thee eastward, and hide thyself by the brook Cherith, that is before Jordan. And it shall be, that thou shalt drink of the brook; and I have commanded the ravens to feed thee there. So he went and did according unto the word of the Lord: for he went and dwelt by the brook Cherith, that is before Jordan. And the ravens brought him bread and flesh in the morning, and bread and flesh in the evening; and drank of the brook" (1 Kings 17:2–6, KJV).

The next story I want to share is about King David, Bathsheba, and Uriah. Uriah was a good and honorable man. He was a soldier in King David's army. Bathsheba was Uriah's wife, whom he loved dearly. One day, King David was out on his roof (while his army was out at battle), and he saw Bathsheba bathing in her own house. He saw her beauty and lusted after her. He summoned her to come to his chamber, and he had sex with her, resulting in her becoming pregnant. Uriah returned from battle, and because others were still fighting in battle, he refused to go to be with his wife. How could he enjoy being with his wife while others were still putting their lives on the line? King David, to rid himself of the guilt of his sin, had Uriah go back to battle, placing him in the front lines of combat where he was ultimately killed. King David had him murdered as a way to cover up his transgression. Nathan, who was a prophet of God, came to David to bring to light this horrible crime and cover-up. To do this, Nathan told David a story:

> And the Lord sent Nathan unto David. And he came unto him, and said unto him. There were two men in one city; the one rich, and the other poor. The rich man had exceeding many flocks and herds: But the poor man had nothing, save one little ewe lamb, which he had bought and nourished up: and it grew up together with him, and with his children; it did eat of his own meat, and drank of his own cup, and lay in his bosom, and was unto him as a daughter. And there came a traveler unto the rich man, and he spared to take of his own flock and of his own herd, to dress for the wayfaring man that was come unto him; but took the poor man's lamb, and dressed it for the man that was come to him. And David's anger was greatly kindled against the man; and he said to Nathan, As the Lord liveth, the man that hath done this thing shall surely die: And he shall restore the lamb fourfold, because he did this thing, and because he had no pity.
>
> And Nathan said to David, Thou art the man. (2 Samuel 12:1–7(a), KJV)

Of all the stories Nathan could have told David, he (or God) chose this one. The poor man loved his little lamb as his own child. The rich man took the poor man's little lamb and slaughtered her for his own merriment. David, being a man after God's own heart (even though his sin was grave), understood the horrid nature of the rich man's crime. David was a shepherd in his youth and cared for many sheep. He had a love and compassion for them and empathetically knew how the poor man must have felt. This story was able to cut through King David's deceit, and he was finally able to face his own transgression.

Let us take a closer look at Jesus. When Jesus came into this world in human form, where did He make His entrance? Of all places, He chose to be born around all of His creatures. God entered creation, and the Word was made flesh. He was born in a stable surrounded by numerous animals. Isn't it interesting that Jesus would choose this plan instead of an inn among sinful people? "And she brought forth her first born son and wrapped him in swaddling clothes, and laid him in a manger, because there was no room for them in the inn" (Luke 2:7, KJV).

Also, some of the first visitors after His birth were the shepherds and their sheep. "And it came to pass, as the angels were gone away from them into heaven, the shepherds said one to another, Let us now go even unto Bethlehem, and see this thing which is come to pass, which the Lord hath made known unto us. And they came with haste, and found Mary and Joseph, and the babe lying in a manger" (Luke 2:15–16, KJV).

The sheep went along with their shepherds on the journey to see the Christ child. Shepherds never leave their sheep unattended. Therefore, all of the sheep were able to witness Jesus coming into the world. There is something definitely significant about all of these scriptures.

St. Francis of Assisi had a passionate belief that all creatures, not just humans, should celebrate the feast of Christmas. Jesus came into the world for all creation, not just humans. St. Francis requested that all people should scatter grains along the roads on Christmas Day for the birds and other animals to have plenty to eat. He also wanted all animals and beasts in the stables to get extra food so all creatures could participate in the celebration of Christmas. St. Francis believed strongly that God was revealing His saving plan for all creatures by having God's Son come into this world in a stable among all the animals.

The Holy Spirit is depicted as a dove coming down from Heaven to land on Jesus: "And John bare record, saying, I saw the Spirit descending from heaven like a dove, and it abode upon him" (John 1:32, KJV). This is also mentioned in Matthew: "And Jesus, when he was baptized, went up straightway out of the water: and, lo, the heavens were opened unto him, and he saw the Spirit of God descending like a dove, and lighting upon him" (Matthew 3:16, KJV). And again in Mark: "And straightway coming up out of the water, he saw the heavens opened, and the Spirit like a dove descending upon him" (Mark 1:10, KJV). Again, animals and birds are intertwined in the message. The Holy Spirit is seen as a dove. God truly is trying to convey our interconnectedness.

The next story I am going to share was quite disturbing to me when I first read it. This story is shared in three of the gospels (Matthew 8:28–34, Mark 5:1–20, and Luke 8:26–39). Demons had possessed a person (or two people as stated in Matthew). Even demons know who Jesus is. The demons requested that Jesus not torment them by sending them out into the abyss but allow them to go into a herd of swine instead:

> And, behold, they cried out, saying, What have we to do with thee, Jesus, thou Son of God? art thou come hither to torment us before the time? And there was a good way off from them an herd of many swine feeding. So the devil besought him, saying, If thou cast us out, suffer us to go away into the herd of

swine. And he said unto them, Go. And when they were come out, they went into the herd of swine: and, behold, the whole herd of swine ran violently down a steep place into the sea, and perished in the waters. (Matthew 8:29–32, KJV)

As I said, this story disturbed me greatly, but then I started to see something that I hadn't initially seen. As soon as the demons entered the pigs, the pigs ran into the sea and drowned. Demons can only have real power when they possess something that is alive. Their power is gone, or at least limited, if they have no living shell to dwell in. The pigs had enough sense to realize they were better off dead than having demons inside of them. Demons can't continue to possess something that is already dead. This story was included in three of the gospels. Again I say God is definitely trying to show us something important. Maybe animals know a little more about the big picture than we humans do.

When Jesus went into Jerusalem toward the end of His human life on this earth, He rode on a donkey. This was done to fulfill prophesy, but don't you think that there may be more to it than that?

"Saying unto them, Go into the village over against you, and straight way ye shall find an ass tied, and a colt with her: loose them, and bring them unto me. And if any man say ought unto you, ye shall say, The Lord hath need of them; and straightway he will send them. All this was done, that it might be fulfilled which was spoken by the prophet, saying, Tell ye the daughter of Sion Behold, the King cometh unto thee, meek, and sitting upon an ass, and a colt the foal of an ass" (Matthew 21:2–5, KJV).

This message is repeated in Luke 19:30–35. Animals are active participants in God's entire plan. When entering Jerusalem on the donkey, a multitude of people congregated around Him, "saying Blessed be the King that cometh in the name of the Lord: peace in heaven, and glory in the highest" (Luke 19:38). Some of the Pharisees told Jesus to make the people stop. Jesus responded to them: "And he answered and said unto them, I tell you that, if these should hold their peace, the stones would immediately cry out" (Luke 19:40, KJV). The stones would cry out! It sounds like Jesus wants us to see that all creation knows Him and worships Him and that He knows every bit of creation very intimately.

Jesus describes Himself as the Good Shepherd. Again, He is linking Himself with His creation. All are intertwined. "I am the good shepherd: the good shepherd giveth his life for the sheep" (John 10:11, KJV). "I am the good shepherd, and know my sheep, and am known of mine. As the Father knoweth me, even so know I the Father: and I lay down my life for the sheep. And other sheep I have, which are not of this fold: them also I must bring, and they shall hear my voice; and there shall be one fold, and one shepherd" (John 10:14–16, KJV).

He doesn't describe Himself as a great king (which He is). He doesn't say He is a mighty warrior. He doesn't even talk about being a wise leader. Instead, He identifies Himself as the Good Shepherd. He cares for His sheep. He knows each one intimately, and each of the sheep knows His voice. I know the sheep are to represent all of us, but I think the meaning is much deeper than that. I believe Jesus is saying that *all* know Him. He is the Good Shepherd for *all* of His creation. "For God is not the author of confusion, but of peace, as in all churches of the saints" (1 Corinthians 14:33). I believe He is being very clear on this matter.

What are some other ways that Jesus is described? In the Gospel of John, Jesus is described as the Lamb of God by John the Baptist: "The next day John seeth Jesus coming unto him, and saith, Behold the Lamb of God, which taketh away the sin of the world" (John 1:29, KJV).

This reference of Jesus being the Lamb of God is repeated frequently in the book of Revelation. Let me share only a couple of examples:

"And I beheld, and, lo, in the midst of the throne and of the four beasts, and in the midst of the elders, stood a Lamb as it had been slain, having seven horns and seven eyes, which are the seven spirits of God sent forth into all the earth" (Revelation 5:6, KJV).

"And when he had taken the book, the four beasts and four and twenty elders fell down before the Lamb, having every one of them harps, and golden vials full of odours, which are the prayers of saints" (Revelation 5:8, KJV).

"Saying with a loud voice, Worthy is the Lamb that was slain to receive power, and riches, and wisdom, and strength, and honour, and glory, and blessing" (Revelation 5:12, KJV).

Cleary, Jesus is the Lamb of God, the ultimate sacrifice to save all of His creation. He is also described as the Lion of the tribe of Judah in a preceding scripture: "And one of the elders saith unto me. Weep not: behold, the Lion of the tribe of Juda, the Root of David, hath prevailed to open the book, and to loose, the seven seals thereof" (Revelation 5:5, KJV). Jesus links Himself with animals. I don't think it is any mistake that He chooses these analogies about Himself.

Let's take a look at some angelic creatures that are portrayed in the Bible. In the book of Genesis we are first introduced to cherubims in the Garden of Eden. "So he drove out the man; and he placed at the east of the garden of Eden Cherubims, and a flaming sword which turned every way, to keep the way of the tree of life" (Genesis 3:24, KJV)

In chapter 25 of the book of Exodus, God instructs Moses on what fashion to make the ark of the covenant. Cherubims would be made of gold and placed on the mercy seat. God would commune with Moses above the mercy seat between the two cherubims. In Exodus 26, God instructs cherubims would be woven into the curtains of the tabernacle and the vail.

Ezekiel from the Old Testament saw these same creatures when he had a vision from God:

> Also out of the midst thereof came the likeness of four living creatures. And this was their appearance; they had the likeness of a man. And every one had four faces, and every one had four wings. And their feet were straight feet; and the sole of their feet was like the sole of a calf's foot: and they sparkled like the colour of burnished brass. And they had the hands of a man under their wings on their four sides; and they four had their faces and their wings. Their wings were joined one to another; they turned not when they went; they went every one straight forward. As for the likeness of their faces, they four had the face of a man, and the face of a lion, on the right side: and they four had the face of an ox on the left side; they four also had the face of an eagle. (Ezekiel 1:5–10, KJV)

Ezekiel sees them again in chapter 10: "And every one had four faces: the first face was the face of a cherub, and the second face was the face of a man, and the third the face of a lion, and the fourth the face of an eagle. And the cherubims were lifted up. This is the living creature that I saw by the river of Chebar" (Ezekiel 10:14–15, KJV).

Isaiah had a vision of another kind of angelic creature. Isaiah had a vision of the Lord sitting upon a throne. He saw creatures in his vision that were called seraphims. In Isaiah 6:2-3 it states: "Above it stood the seraphims: each one had six wings; with twain he covered his face, and with twain he covered his feet, and with twain he did fly. And one cried unto another, and said, Holy, holy, holy, is the Lord of hosts: the whole earth is full of his glory" (KJV).

These creatures are portrayed again in the book of Revelation. In the book of Revelation, four beasts are described around the throne of God:

> And before the throne there was a sea of glass like unto crystal: and in the midst of the throne; and round about the throne, were four beast full of eyes before and behind. And the first beast was like a lion, and the second beast like a calf, and the third beast had a face as a man, and the fourth beast was like a flying eagle. And the four beasts had each of them six wings about him; and they were full of eyes within: and they rest not day or night, saying Holy, holy, holy, Lord God Almighty, which was, and is, and is to come (Revelation 4:6-8, KJV).

After these four beasts, or seraphims, sing praises to the Lord, the twenty-four elders fall down before Jesus and say, "Thou art worthy, O Lord, to receive glory and honour and power: for thou hast created all things, and for thy pleasure they are and were created" (Revelation 4:11, KJV).

Both of these angelic creatures, cherubims and seraphims, sound similar to each other. They both have characteristics of animals, of birds, and of humans. I find this very interesting. They were made by God this way for some important reason. These angelic creatures play a very important and consistent part in the entire Bible from Genesis through

Revelation. The cherubims were even incorporated in the tabernacle and portrayed in a golden image on the mercy seat of the ark of the covenant. It was between the two golden cherubims God would be between when he would commune with Moses. We may not understand all of this now, but someday we will.

One more verse that I believe is very telling about the interconnection of all God's creatures is in chapter 5 of Revelation, the animals all praise Jesus: "And every creature which is in heaven, and on the earth, and under the earth, and such as are in the sea, and all that are in them, heard I saying, Blessing, and honour, and glory, and power, be unto him that sitteth upon the throne, and unto the Lamb for ever and ever" (Revelation 5:13, KJV).

We have covered many scriptures that share creatures' involvement in the message of God from Genesis to Revelation. What can we learn from all of this? Animals are receptive to the spiritual world. They can see things that we humans cannot. All creatures hear God's voice and obey Him. God also uses them as examples of true trust in the Lord. Even though Jesus is the King of Kings and Lord of all, He doesn't make a huge point of this. He doesn't portray Himself as a great warrior or hunter but rather a God of peace and love. He is the Good Shepherd that is willing to lay down His life to save and protect His sheep. Jesus is interconnected with all of His creatures. He is so connected that He calls Himself the Good Shepherd, the Lamb of God, and the Lion of the tribe of Judah. He chooses to portray Himself in an animal form and as caretaker of all creatures. These aren't beautiful analogies to sound poetic; there is a much deeper and richer meaning behind them.

God is desperately crying out to all of us to show the true meaning of His word. He wants us to see how we are all interconnected and are all part of something much greater than we can understand. Let's look at recent examples of this interconnection. There are countless stories of animals saving people from death. Animals have informed their owners of a fire or sought out help when a loved one has fallen due to heart attack, stroke, seizure, or some kind of accident. Without the animal's intervention, the person would have surely died. I heard a story of a little pig going out into the road and playing dead in order to get someone to stop. When someone finally stopped, she led the person into the home where her owner was found in a medical crisis. The person was then able to call 911. That act of love by the pig saved her owner's life. Another story was about a little boy who got lost in the woods. The weather was very cold. A pack of dogs found the boy and lay with him and on top of him to keep him warm until he was found by the authorities. If those dogs had not lain over the boy, he would have surely died due to hypothermia. There are countless stories of animals saving lives. We could go on and on with examples of their heroic actions.

Animals are used to help physically ill and emotionally disturbed children. They are able to reach these people in a way that no therapy otherwise could. The positive effects have been nothing short of phenomenal. Animals are used to help the elderly, which has shown to decrease depression and extend their life span and quality of life. Dogs are trained to help the physically disabled. The trained dogs help their owners to function in society and live independently. We cannot dismiss the important role animals have had on our physical, mental, emotional, and spiritual well-being.

There are countless books on the subject of animal miracle stories and their positive effects on humans. There are even programs on television that are dedicated to sharing animal miracle stories. On one such program, I saw a story about two deer hunters finding a poor deer stranded out on a frozen lake. They had compassion for the little deer and spent hours attempting to rescue her. Once they finally got her to safe ground, they let her go. She got up, walked a few paces, and then turned around and looked at the two men for a long moment before she turned back around and ran off. Something magical happened to these two deer hunters. Their hearts melted, and they chose to never go deer hunting again. What a story! It happens all the time. How can we explain it? These testimonies cannot be dismissed as coincidence or a stroke of good luck—not with the numerous accounts of this phenomena occurring. Animals have a true love for their owners, a love that surpasses our understanding. It is like God's love—unconditional. I also believe that it points to God's communication with animals and our ultimate interconnection with all creation. Maybe animals are really messengers of God sent from heaven to teach us what true love is all about. The one thing that cannot be disputed is that animals have an uncanny way of knowing things and doing things that goes beyond our understanding.

This is a dance that God does with us, animals, and all creation. He is desperately trying to show us how we are all interconnected and interrelated. We are all intertwined, humans and creatures, all interwoven and linked together in a beautiful tapestry. Without one or the other, things would be out of balance. It takes all of creation to keep the balance and the true beauty. God is whole and complete. His design is whole and perfect. God is calling out to all of us to join in the beautiful, graceful dance with Him, and He is the master choreographer.

Dear Beloved Jesus, our Savior,

You are the Lamb and the Lion. You were torn and broken for us.

You were made whole and alive to make us whole and alive.

Please help us all to see the world and all creation as you see it:

Through Your eyes with Your purpose and Your plan for all things.

Amen.

Luke's Story

photo taken by Suzy Mast-Lee

The youth group at church has a yard sale every year as a fund-raising project. It takes place in early August to correspond with a citywide celebration. On the Saturday during the celebration, the town has a big parade with floats, the town's school band, fancy cars, and so on. It is your basic hometown parade. We have chosen to hold the yard sale during this time because the parade route goes right by the church. Crowds of people stand on the church grounds in order to have a good view of the parade. Those people tend to then come and shop at the yard sale. Oh well, it works.

This story isn't about the yard sale, but I needed to let you know what was going on to set the stage for this story. The parade was getting lined up to pass by. I noticed a big dog running through the church grounds. He was a huge, dark brown and white short-haired dog. He went to the basement door of the church, and if it had been opened, he would have gone on in. He looked around and then ran down the street (one that was not on the parade route). I said a little prayer for his safety and then went on with the work I was doing. Not too long after he ran off, he came back around. He seemed nervous and kept running from here to there. He went over to a ditch at the corner of two roads where the parade was getting ready to start. It had rained heavily the night before, and there was rain water in the ditch. The dog started lapping up the water. I took a closer look at him and noticed how terribly skinny he was. I took a donut that we had for the kids to eat that morning (and I know it probably wasn't good what I was about to do) and went over to the dog and offered him pieces of the donut. At first he seemed a little uncertain of it, but then he came over and gobbled it down. I had a helper watch him while I went into the church to get some more water. When I came back with the water, he lapped it up.

I needed to find out where he belonged. He had a collar on but no ID tags. The parade was beginning to start, and I was afraid this dog would get scared and start to run, possibly getting trampled by the parade. Plus, one block to the north of us was a highway. If he started to run in that direction, the results could be fatal. I didn't have a leash, so I made something that could serve as one with a couple of belts we had at the yard sale. Sometimes you just have to get creative. I started off in one direction where I saw some people out in their yard. They had never seen the dog before. While I was looking for someone else outside that I could ask, Animal Control came cruising by. The Animal Control person, whose name was Lisa, said she knew Luke, the dog, and his owner. She had had to pick him up numerous times before. I got her card, and she said it was okay to call and check on whether his owner picked him up or not. Since apparently this had happened numerous times, she was going to fine the owner. I said a prayer for Luke's safety.

Apparently Luke's owner did come to pick him up. Luke had apparently had numerous close calls. Animal Control had to pick him up when he was running around the highway! I prayed daily for Luke and for God to keep him safe. I worried that he would get loose again and would not be so lucky. Plus, I began to wonder what he was he running away from. It wasn't looking like he had a very good place; otherwise why would he constantly be trying to leave? Anyway, all I could do was pray. God can do all things, and I knew He could look out for Luke.

Two weeks later, my husband and I were attempting to do the dreaded thing that we had put off for too long. We were attempting to balance our checkbook. We don't spend money on frivolous stuff, but we still end up spending more than we make. A lot of our money goes for all our animals. With food, vet bills, medicines, and the like, it adds up quite fast. It seemed we were in such a big hole we had no idea how we would ever get out of it. We were brainstorming ways to help us out of this big landslide we found ourselves in. Needing a break, we decided to take the dogs outside. Just as we let them out, the phone rang. He went in to answer it. He joined me outside a short time later, and he had an unsettled look on his face. I asked him what was wrong, and he said, "That was Lisa, the Animal Control lady. She has had to pick up Luke three to four times over the past two weeks. His owner asked her if she knew anyone who would want Luke. She asked if we were interested and whether she could give his owner our phone number. I told her I had to talk with you and would call her back."

What were we going to do? We really didn't have the money to take on another dog. We were struggling with the ones we had. Then we processed the issue that we really hadn't talked about. All of our dogs have names from the Bible. We have Noah Simon, Jonah Isaac, and Hannah Ruth. Of all names this dog could have had, his name was Luke! Was this a sign from God? Did He want us to take him? Even though we had no money, we didn't want to say no to God. Then I thought of the story in the Bible about Elijah and the woman and her son. After a big drought in the land, Elijah was told by the Lord to go to Zarephath and that there was a woman there who would take him in. He did as the Lord told him and found the woman gathering sticks. He asked her to give him a drink of water and to fix a cake for him. She told him that she only had a handful of meal and a little oil, which she was going to fix for her and her son and then they were going to die. She had nothing to give and didn't have enough to take care of her and her son. He asked her to go ahead and make the food, giving him some first. She ended up doing as he asked, and her meal and her oil never ran out. She ended up acting out of faith instead of common sense, and that made all the difference. Was this what God wanted from us? We had nothing to give and could hardly take care of our own, yet did God want us to do this anyway? We called Lisa back and said to go ahead and give Luke's owner our number.

The story doesn't end there. In fact, what happened next confirmed what we had to do. That Saturday we had youth group. We had to pick up one of the girls on our way to church. When she got into our car, she asked, "What is wrong with your phone?" We responded that we didn't think anything was wrong with it. She went on to say that she had been trying to reach us since Friday night but every time she called the phone wouldn't ring. We had gotten the call from Lisa, the Animal Control lady, that morning, so of course our phone was working. She must have made a mistake and misdialed our number. When we got to church, we tried to call home. The phone wouldn't ring; our phone was not working. Later that afternoon when we got home, we checked our phone again. There was a dial tone. I called Pop to have him call. I waited and nothing happened. I called him back, and he said he tried but it wouldn't ring. Our phone wasn't working. It had rained a great deal, so I wondered if that was the culprit and affecting the phone line. And then the big question surfaced: Why was it that with all the people who had tried to reach us and had failed, the one call that had come through was from Lisa, the Animal Control lady, who called about Luke? This was definitely a bizarre quandary. We looked at each other and believed that this was an act of God and we had to be willing to take in Luke, trusting God to help us out with the money issue.

I picked up Luke from Animal Control. He was even skinnier than the first time I saw him. He literally looked like a skeleton with skin stretched over it. Lisa even commented on her concern about him and his health. I found out that he was a German short-haired pointer. He apparently had been trained as a hunting dog. Well, he wouldn't be using any of those skills anymore. Lisa made the comment when I went with her out to the pen to get Luke that it seemed that he remembered me. She let me take him without paying any fee. Another God thing?

Probably. Lisa shared that Luke had been abused and that the other dog that he lived with was allowed to torment and bully him. Not a good situation at all. So that was what Luke was running from. He wouldn't have that with us. Our goal is to have a peaceable kingdom.

Luke had a few problems adjusting to life at Funky Farm at first but finally adapted quite well to his new home. Luke no longer is skin and bones but now looks healthy as he should be. I guess I didn't realize when I kept praying to God for Him to keep Luke safe that God would call on me to be a part of that process. That's okay, though. God answered my prayer. Luke Micah is safe, cared for, healthy, and truly happy. And above all, somehow, some way, we are still paying the bills, and the kids haven't gone hungry.

The Promise

We discussed in an earlier chapter the covenant that God made with Noah and his family and all creatures. He will never destroy the earth with a great flood again. God gave the rainbow as a sign of remembrance of that covenant that He made. In this chapter I want to focus on another covenant that God foretells that He will make with humans and all creatures. Hosea 2:18 says, "And in that day will I make a covenant for them with the beast of the field and with the fowls of heaven, and with the creeping things of the ground: and I will break the bow and the sword and the battle out of the earth, and will make them lie down safely" (KJV).

God is sharing about a covenant He will make with man and nature. We are reminded again that we have a kinship with our fellow creatures. We are all intertwined together, and God promises that He will make peace prevail with all of His creation. The prophet Isaiah refers numerous times to God's plan of a peaceable kingdom:

> The wolf also shall dwell with the lamb, and the leopard shall lie down with the kid: and the calf and the young lion and the fatling together: and a little child shall lead them. And the cow

and the bear shall feed; their young ones shall lie down together: and the lion shall eat straw like the ox. And the sucking child shall play on the hole of the asp, and the weaned child shall put his hand on the cockatrice' den. They shall not hurt nor destroy in all my holy mountain: for the earth shall be full of the knowledge of the Lord, as the waters cover the sea. (Isaiah 11:6–9, KJV)

God promises that all will live in peace. There will be neither hurting nor destroying. The entire land will be "full of the knowledge of the Lord." God gives a crystal-clear message of His desire and His plan. Just a side note: no one will be eating flesh anymore. All will become vegetarian as was His plan at the origin of this earth. Let us not overlook the very important point God is sharing about His plan for all creation. In this passage He goes into detail about the nature of animals and the interconnection with the child leading them. This same message is repeated in a condensed form toward the end of the book of Isaiah: "The wolf and the lamb shall feed together, and the lion shall eat straw like the bullock: and dust shall be the serpent's meat. They shall not hurt nor destroy in all my holy mountain, saith the Lord" (Isaiah 65:25, KJV).

God is definitely trying to let us know something very important. He doesn't repeat Himself for no reason. God has a plan that is much grander than we can even comprehend. God loves humans. He made them in His own image. God also passionately loves all of His creatures. He is making that emphatically clear in these scriptures.

God gives us a picture of everything coming full circle: how everything was meant to be it ultimately will be in the end. Man's sin corrupted the earth and all that dwells in it. God gives us the promise that He will make things all new.

"Remember ye not the former things, neither consider the things of old. Behold, I will do a new thing, now it shall spring forth; shall ye not know it? I will even make a way in the wilderness, and rivers in the desert. The beast of the field shall honour me, the dragons and the owls: because I give waters in the wilderness, and rivers in the desert to give drink to my people, my chosen" (Isaiah 43:18:20, KJV).

"Lift up your eyes to the heavens and look upon the earth beneath: for the heavens shall vanish away like smoke, and the earth shall wax old like a garment and they that dwell therein shall die in like manner: but my salvation shall be forever, and my righteousness shall not be abolished" (Isaiah 51:6, KJV).

"For, behold, I create new heavens and a new earth: and the former shall not be remembered, nor come into mind" (Isaiah 65:17, KJV).

And then God adds, again, how all will come to worship Him: "And it shall come to pass, that from one new moon to another, and from one sabbath to another, shall all flesh come to worship before me, saith the Lord" (Isaiah 66:32, KJV).

God continues to repeat Himself, and the message remains the same. All flesh (all means all) will worship Him. God will make everything new and perfect. All creatures will live in peace together. To me, it sounds like things will go back to being like the Garden of Eden, except evil will not intrude into it. Sin will be blotted out. The peace that God always intended will be for ever and ever. That's a promise I hold very close to my heart. I can trust in God, because unlike humans, He never breaks a promise.

The Ugly Truth:
The True Meaning of Sacrifice

It seems like we are such a long way from God's promise of a peaceful kingdom. Look around at our world today. There is so much violence: crime, murder, rape, destruction, cruelty, fighting—the list goes on and on. It is difficult to trust others. We don't feel safe in our communities and sometimes not even in our own homes. Schools are no longer safe places to send our kids. Violence happens anywhere and everywhere. Why is that? Here, in such a technically advanced time, when we think we are such highly sophisticated people, we still have so much evil. The bottom line is we do not learn. Times were also bad during the times when the Bible was written. Really, things haven't changed much. We still want what we want and don't care who gets hurt in the process. We think of ourselves instead of others. I don't mean to come across as pessimistic, but we need to face the facts and as I stated at the beginning of this, I want the truth. Sometimes the truth hurts. Man is essentially evil. Let us explore a few scriptures that reveal God's concern about our dismal state.

Dwila R. Funk

"The earth also was corrupt before God, and the earth was filled with violence. And God looked upon the earth, and, behold, it was corrupt; for all flesh had corrupted his way upon the earth" (Genesis 6:11–12, KJV).

"Vanity of vanities, saith the Preacher, vanity of vanities, all is vanity" (Ecclesiastes 1:2, KJV).

In the above scripture, King Solomon is sharing his concern about our state of being. Our priorities are for vain things or foolishness filled with emptiness.

"How long shall the land mourn, and the herbs of every field wither, for the wickedness of them that dwell therein? the beasts are consumed, and the birds; because they said, He shall not see our last end" (Jeremiah 12:4, KJV).

"They have made it desolate, and being desolate it mourneth unto me; the whole land is made desolate, because no man layeth it to heart" (Jeremiah 12:11, KJV).

"The heart is deceitful above all things, and desperately wicked: who can know it?" (Jeremiah 17:9, KJV).

"For every kind of beasts, and of birds, and of serpents, and of things of the sea, is tamed, and hath been tamed of mankind: But the tongue can no man tame; it is un unruly evil, full of deadly poison" (James 3:7–8, KJV).

God appointed leaders over His people to help guide them in the right path. The problem was that a lot of those leaders also became corrupt in their own thinking and actions. God appointed prophets to speak God's truth:

> Son of man, prophesy against the shepherds of Israel, prophesy, and say unto them, Thus saith the Lord God unto the shepherds; Woe be to the shepherds of Israel that do feed themselves!

Should not the shepherds feed the flock? Ye eat the fat, and ye clothe you with the wool, ye kill them that are fed: but ye feed not the flock. The diseased have ye not strengthened, neither have ye healed that which was sick, neither have ye bound up that which was broken, neither have ye brought again that which was driven away, neither have ye sought that which was lost, but with force and with cruelty have ye ruled them.

And they were scattered, because there is no shepherd: and they became meat to all the beasts of the field, when they were scattered. My sheep wandered through all the mountains, and upon every high hill: Yea, my flock was scattered upon all the face of the earth and none did search or seek after them. Therefore, ye shepherds, hear the word of the Lord; As I live, saith the Lord God, surely because my flock became a prey, and my flock became meat to every beast of the field, because there was no shepherd, neither did my shepherds search for my flock, but the shepherds fed themselves, and fed not my flock, Therefore, O ye shepherds, hear the word of the Lord: Thus saith the Lord God; Behold I am against the shepherds; and I will require my flock at their hand, and cause them to cease from feeding the flock; neither shall the shepherds feed themselves anymore; for I will deliver my flock from their mouth, that they may not be meat for them. (Ezekiel 34:2–10, KJV)

"Thus saith the Lord my God; Feed the flock of the slaughter; whose possessors slay them, and hold themselves not guilty: and they that sell them say, Blessed be the Lord; for I am rich: and their own shepherds pity them not" (Zechariah 11:4–5, KJV).

The leaders were consumed with their own self-importance, thinking that they knew more about God than they really did. These leaders became more associated with the world's ways rather than God's ways.

Humans continued to sin, even the leaders. They thought of themselves and didn't take care of each other. It wasn't much different from today. God is holy. We, by a long shot, are not. To get close to God, the sin factor stands in the way. Now is the time when we must address the issue of animal sacrifices. I really do dislike this part, but to get to where we are going, we have to pass this part of the journey. I am going to explain the issue of sacrifice the best way I can, so it will be in very simple terms because that is the only way I can understand it myself. Because humans are sinful, there had to be some mechanism, if you will, to clean them up to be near God. Animals are sinless. Innocent blood (blood being the life force in all of us) had to be shed to wash away the sins, thus cleaning them up. I know this sounds gross, but that is how I understand it. The people of Israel would bring the best animal they had to give to God to atone for their sins. The priests took care of the sacrifice, and the blood would be drained from the limp body. Thank the good Lord we don't have to do that now. The problem came when they would continue to do the sacrifices but their hearts didn't change. They would continue down the same road. When it was time to do another sacrifice, they would get another one of their little animals and take it to be offered up to God, think everything was okay again, and go along their merry way. That isn't what God wanted. He wanted a change in spirit, a change of the heart, and a change in behavior. Sacrifices became routine.

Take a moment to think about your own life. Are there things you do that have become routine and the meaning has been lost somewhere in the process? Let's take, for example, going to church every week. Do you ever think as long as you go to church on Sunday you have done your duty for God, but when attending the service you're not even paying attention to the message? Maybe you listen to the message while you're at church, but as soon as you leave the building, the message leaves you too? What about reciting the Lord's Prayer? Do you listen to the words and meditate on their meaning, or are they just a string of memorized words that can be recited by automatic pilot? I am not trying to cast stones at anyone. I can be just as guilty as the next person. All I am trying to say is that it may be wise for us to look at what we do and let there be meaning in it.

God was not pleased with what the people were doing. He didn't want a lot of animals dying needlessly. He sent His prophets to share His message and His desire. I don't know if anybody really listened. I hope we do.

"Sacrifice and offering thou didst not desire; mine ears hast thou opened: burnt offerings and sin offerings hast thou not required" (Psalm 40:6, KJV).

> Hear, O my people, and I will speak, O Israel, and I will testify against thee: I am God, even thy God. I will not reprove thee for thy sacrifices or thy burnt offerings, to have been continually before me. I will take no bullock out of thy house, nor he goats out of thy folds. For every beast of the forest is mine, and the cattle upon a thousand hills. I know all the fowls of the mountains: and the wild beasts of the field are mine. If I were hungry, I would not tell thee: for the world is mine, and the fullness there of. Will I eat the flesh of bulls or drink the blood of goats? (Psalm 50:7–12, KJV)

"For thou desirest not sacrifice: else would I give it: thou delightest not in burnt offering. The sacrifices of God are a broken spirit: a broken and contrite heart. O God, thou wilt not despise" (Psalm 51:16–17, KJV).

> To what purpose is the multitude of your sacrifices unto me? saith the Lord: I am full of the burnt offerings of rams, and the fat of fed beasts; and I delight not in the blood of bullocks, or of lambs, or of he goats. When ye come to appear before me, who hath required this at your hand, to tread my courts? Bring no more vain oblations; incense is an abomination unto me; the new moons and sabbaths, the calling of assemblies, I cannot away with; it is iniquity, even the solemn meeting. Your new moons and your appointed feasts my soul hateth: they are a trouble unto me; I am weary to bear them. And when ye spread forth your hands, I will hide mine eyes from you: yea, when ye make many prayers, I will not hear: your hands are full of blood. Wash you, make you clean; put away the evil of your doings from before mine eyes; cease to do evil; Learn to do well; seek judgment, relieve the oppressed, judge the fatherless, plead for the widow. (Isaiah 1:11–17, KJV)

> Thus saith the Lord of hosts, the God of Israel; Put your burnt offerings unto your sacrifices, and eat flesh. For I spake not unto your fathers, nor commanded them in the day that I brought them out of the land of Egypt, concerning burnt offerings or sacrifices: But this thing commanded I them, saying, Obey my voice, and I will be your God, and ye shall be my people: and walk ye in all the ways that I have commanded you, that it may be well unto you. But they hearkened not, nor inclined their ear, but walked in the counsels and in the imagination of their evil heart, and went backward, and not forward. Since the day that

your fathers came forth out of the land of Egypt unto this day I have even sent unto you all my servants the prophets, daily rising up early and sending them: Yet they hearkened not unto me, nor inclined their ear, but hardened their neck: they did worse than their fathers. Therefore thou shalt speak all these words unto them; but they will not hearken to thee: thou shalt also call unto them; but they will not answer thee. But thou shalt say unto them, This is a nation that obeyeth not the voice of the Lord their God, nor receiveth correction: truth is perished, and is cut off from their mouth. (Jeremiah 7:21–28, KJV)

"For I desired mercy, and not sacrifice; and the knowledge of God more than burnt offerings" (Hosea 6:6, KJV).

"I have written to him the great things of my law, but they were counted as a strange thing. They sacrifice flesh for the sacrifices of mine offerings, and eat it; but the Lord accepteth them not; now will he remember their iniquity and visit their sins: they shall return to Egypt" (Hosea 8:12–13, KJV).

"I hate, I despise your feast days, and I will not smell in your solemn assemblies. Though ye offer me burnt offerings and your meat offerings, I will not accept them: neither will I regard the peace offerings of your fat beasts. Take thou away from me the noise of thy songs; for I will not hear the melody of thy viols. But let judgment run down as waters, and righteousness as a mighty stream. Have ye offered unto me sacrifices and offerings in the wilderness forty years, O house of Israel?" (Amos 5:21–25, KJV).

"Wherewith shall I come before the Lord, and bow myself before the high God? Shall I come before him with burnt offerings, with calves of a year old? Will the Lord be pleased with thousands of rams, or with ten thousands of rivers of oil? Shall I give my first born for my transgressions, the fruit of my body for the sin of my soul? He hath shewed thee, O man, what is good; and what doth the Lord require of thee, but to do justly, and to love mercy, and to walk humbly with thy God?" (Micah 6:6–8, KJV).

God didn't want all those animal sacrifices. In fact, He was getting pretty sick of them. The act was becoming a ritual and the meaning behind it had been lost. The prophets spell out what God really requires. He wants all of us to sacrifice ourselves—our wills, our hearts, our thoughts—and surrender to His will. God wants us to listen to His voice and walk in His ways. The initial sinful trait remains deeply imbedded in all of us. It was there with the Israelites, and it still remains there today in us. We need to get rid of our arrogance and conceit and realize that we are nothing without God. If we could truly become totally humble before God, we would find that we are everything to Him. All He asks for is that we put Him first, be kind and loving to each other and all His creation. If we could do that, everything would fall into place, but for some reason that always seems too hard and complicated for us to take in.

Jesus voiced clearly His concerns. God's house wasn't a house of worship anymore. People had corrupted it. The leaders were not good, godly leaders. As stated earlier, they had become corrupted by the world's ways.

"And he taught, saying unto them, Is it not written, My house shall be called of all nations the house of prayer? but ye have made it a den of thieves. And the scribes, and chief priests, heard it, and sought how they might destroy him: for they feared him, because all the people was astonished at his doctrine" (Mark 11:17–18, KJV).

Because the scribes and the chief priests were threatened by Jesus's preaching, they wanted to destroy Him. Isn't that the common theme?

Covering up deceit and guilt doesn't make it go away. God not only judges our actions but also knows our hearts.

In the next scripture, Jesus was going into Jerusalem during the Passover. He became upset with what was going on. Now remember, He didn't want all the animal sacrifices as we have already talked about. He was also upset, though, about how they were going about it. People had brought animals there to sell to others who needed something to sacrifice. People could go to the temple, purchase an animal or a dove, and take it to be sacrificed for their sins. The people hadn't changed, but now they had also gotten lazy about it. It wasn't like they were giving anything of themselves; they were buying their forgiveness. And to top it off, some people were making money off of it!

"And Jews' Passover was at hand, and Jesus went up to Jerusalem, and found in the temple those that sold oxen and sheep and doves, and the changers of money sitting: And when he had made a scourge of small cords, he drove them all out of the temple, and the sheep, and the oxen: and poured out the changers' money, and overthrew the tables: And said unto them that sold doves, Take these things hence; make not my Father's house an house of merchandise" (John 2:13–16, KJV).

Jesus reiterated the messages of the prophets. Still, few wanted to see the truth. Will we also remain unchanged?

"But go ye and learn what that meaneth, I will have mercy, and not sacrifice: for I am not come to call the righteous, but sinners to repentance" (Matthew 9:13, KJV).

"But if ye had known what this meaneth, I will have mercy, and not sacrifice, ye would not have condemned the guiltless" (Matthew 12:7, KJV).

People didn't listen to God; they didn't listen to the prophets; and when God came down to earth in human form (incarnate), they still didn't listen. The truth has always been there. God beckons us to see and be led by His truth. Will we hear His call?

> For the wrath of God is revealed from heaven against all ungodliness and unrighteousness of men, who hold the truth in unrighteousness; Because that which may be known of God is manifest in them; for God hath shewed it unto them. For the invisible things of him from the creation of the world are clearly seen, being understood by the things that are made, even his eternal power and Godhead; so that they are without excuse: Because that, when they knew God, they glorified him not as God, neither were thankful; but became vain in their imaginations, and their foolish heart was darkened. Professing themselves to be wise, they became fools, And changed the glory of the uncorruptible God into an image made like to corruptible man, and to birds, and fourfooted beasts, and creeping things. (Romans 1:18–23, KJV)

The Bridge

Because people were not getting the message of what God wanted from them (they weren't even paying attention to the prophets that God sent), there had to be another way. God, being the God that He is, knew that we humans would screw up. Actually, He knew it back in the Garden of Eden, so He already had a plan in the waiting. God came down to earth in human form—incarnate. Jesus humbled Himself to become a living example to teach us what God really wanted and became the ultimate sacrifice once and for all for sin. Jesus made a new covenant that bridged the gap between all of us (including creation) and God.

Before we go further, I want to share a story I heard a DJ tell on a Christian radio program that was being broadcast during the middle of the night years ago. Sometimes I have problems sleeping, so I get to hear interesting things in the wee hours of the night that I otherwise might have missed. I don't remember who the DJ was or where it was broadcast from, but the story burned into my heart, and I never have forgotten it. It helped me realize and understand more clearly this wonderful thing Jesus did for us. I also liked it because it was about a man and his concern for some birds that were in need of saving. The story goes something like this. There was a man and his wife who lived just outside of a small town. They had a little bit of land and a barn. It was Christmas Eve. The man was not a Christian, but his wife was. His wife was planning to go to Christmas Eve service at the country church she attended, which was close to their home. She asked her husband if he wanted to go with her to the Christmas Eve service. He didn't understand this whole Christian tradition. How could Jesus Christ be both man and God at the same time? It just made no sense to him. He declined his wife's invitation: "No, honey, you go on to church. I plan to read this book that I've been planning to read." She left, and he settled down into his chair to read his book. All of a sudden he heard the wind pick up outside and heard a *thud, thud, thud* on the family-room window. He quickly went outside to see what was going on. There was a storm coming, and the wind was blowing wildly. He then saw what was hitting up against the front windows. There were several birds all flying around in a cluster, scared and probably disoriented and frantic due to the upcoming storm and wind. The man's heart went out to these little birds, and he wanted to help them. He thought, *If they went into the barn, they would be safe and out of the storm.* He went out to the barn to open the door and turn on the light, hoping they would see it and go to the light. The birds continued to whirl around frantically, hitting up against the window of the house. They didn't seem to notice the shelter waiting for them. The man tried to lead them to the barn, but it didn't work. He went into the barn and got some birdseed. He thought, *If I make a trail of bird seed to the barn, they will follow it and go into the safety of the barn.* He laid out seed from the birds to the barn. The birds didn't even notice the seeds and continued in their frantic state. The man was feeling desperate, discouraged, and helpless. *Oh, if I could just become a bird for awhile, I could lead them to safety.* Just then the bells on the church rang out. The man heard the bells and fell on his knees. "God, now I understand." To me, this story gives a tangible example of why Jesus did what He did for us. I just had to share it with you. Now we need to press on with our exploration of the old versus the new covenant.

What happened to make the old ways obsolete? I found that in the book of Hebrews, the apostle Paul explains about the new and better covenant. Let me share a few verses that helped me understand. Actually, I would recommend reading Hebrews chapters 8–10 if you would like to understand more about the old covenant versus the new covenant and the ineffectiveness of sacrifices. For the sake of time and space, I will only share a few verses to highlight the main points:

"For if that first covenant had been faultless, then should no place have been sought for the second" (Hebrews 8:7, KJV).

"In that he saith, A new covenant, he hath made the first old. Now that which decayeth and waxeth old is ready to vanish away" (Hebrews 8:13, KJV).

> But Christ being come an high priest of good things to come, by a greater and more perfect tabernacle, not made with hands, that is to say, not of this building; Neither by the blood of goats and calves, but by his own blood he entered in once into the holy place, having obtained eternal redemption for us. For if the blood of bulls and of goats, and the ashes of an heifer sprinkling the unclean, sanctifieth to the purifying of the flesh: How much more shall the blood of Christ, who through the eternal Spirit offered himself without spot to God, purge your conscience from dead works to serve the living God? And for this cause he is the mediator of the new testament, that by means of death, for the redemption of the transgressions that were under the first testament, they which are called might receive the promise of eternal inheritance. (Hebrews 9:11–15, KJV)

"So Christ was once offered to bear the sins of many; and unto them that look for him shall he appear the second time without sin unto salvation" (Hebrews 9:28, KJV).

"For the law having a shadow of good things to come, and not the very image of the things, can never with those sacrifices which they offered year by year continually make the comers thereunto perfect. For then would they not have ceased to be offered? because that the worshippers once purged should have had no more conscience of sins. But in those sacrifices there is a remembrance again made of sins every year. For it is not possible that the blood of bulls and of goats should take away sins. Wherefore when he cometh into the world, he saith, Sacrifice and offering thou wouldest not, but a body hast thou prepared me: In burnt offerings and sacrifices for sin thou hast had no pleasure. Then said I, Lo, I come (in the volume of the book it is written of me,) to do thy will, O God. Above when he said, Sacrifice and offering and burnt offerings and offering for sin thou wouldest not, neither hadst pleasure therein; which are offered by the law; Then said he, Lo, I come to do thy will, O God. He taketh away the first, that he may establish the second. By the which will we are sanctified through the offering of the body of Jesus Christ once for all. And every priest standeth daily ministering and offering oftentimes the same sacrifices, which can never take away sins: But this man, after he had offered one sacrifice for sins for ever, sat down on the right hand of God; From henceforth expecting till his enemies be made his footstool. For by one offering he hath perfected for ever them that are sanctified. Whereof the Holy Ghost also is a witness to us: for after that he had said before, This is the covenant that I will make with them after those days, saith the Lord, I will put my laws into their hearts, and in their minds will I write them; And their sins and iniquities will I remember no more. Now where remission of these is, there is no more offering for sin. (Hebrews 10:1–18, KJV)

Jesus Christ the same yesterday, and today, and forever. Be not carried about with divers and strange doctrines. For it is a good thing that the heart be established with grace; not with meats, which not profited them that have been occupied therein. We have an altar, whereof they have no right to eat which serve the tabernacle. For the bodies of those beasts, whose blood is brought into the sanctuary by the high priest for sin, are burned without the camp. Wherefore Jesus also, that he might sanctify the people with his own blood, suffered without the gate. Let us go forth therefore unto him without the camp, bearing his reproach. For here have we no continuing city, but we seek one to come. By him therefore let us offer the sacrifice of praise to God continually, that is, the fruit of our lips giving thanks to his name. But to do good and to communicate forget not: for with such sacrifices God is well pleased. (Hebrews 13:8–16, KJV)

God decided to come down to earth in the form of man to show us the way. Jesus came to walk us through this wilderness we live in. He came down from heaven to be slaughtered for all of our sins in order to make a new and permanent way to be with Him. He made the new covenant and sacrificed Himself to end all sacrifices.

"The next day John seeth Jesus coming unto him; and saith, Behold the Lamb of God, which taketh away the sin of the world" (John 1:29, KJV).

"For God so loved the world, that he gave his only begotten Son, that whosoever believeth in him should not perish, but have everlasting life" (John 3:16, KJV).

> I am the good shepherd, and know my sheep, and am known of mine. As the Father knoweth me, even so know I the Father: and I lay down my life for the sheep. And other sheep I have, which are not of this fold: them also I must bring and they shall hear my voice; and there shall be one fold, and one shepherd. Therefore doth my Father love me, because I lay down my life, that I might take it again. No man taketh it from me, but I lay it down of myself. I have power to lay it down, and I have power to take it again. This commandment have I received of my Father. (John 10:14–18, KJV)

The old covenant passed away and Jesus made all things new. Jesus made a bridge for us to get to God. "Jesus saith unto him, I am the way, the truth, and the life: no man cometh unto the Father, but by me" (John 14:6, KJV).

He is the bridge to eternal life and heaven. "Jesus said unto her, I am the resurrection, and the life: he that believeth in me, though he were dead, yet shall he live: And whosoever liveth and believeth in me shall never die. Believest thou this?" (John 11:25–26, KJV).

This bridge is not only for us, but for all creatures and creation itself. In Luke 3:4–6, John the Baptist says,

"As it is written in the book of the words of Esaias the prophet, saying, the voice of one crying in the wilderness, prepare ye the way of the Lord, make his paths straight. Every valley shall be filled, and every mountain and hill shall be brought low; and the crooked shall be made straight, and the rough ways shall be made smooth; *and all flesh shall see the salvation of God"* (KJV, emphasis added).

"And all flesh shall see the salvation of God." Let us not miss this. It doesn't say only humans but all flesh. All flesh means what it says. We have seen no distinctions in the scriptures. The next scripture we will look at gives a clear description of what has happened and what will be. It sums up the questions about all of God's creatures' fate and God's plan. Look at it very closely:

"For I reckon that the sufferings of this present time are not worthy to be compared with the glory which shall be revealed in us. *For the earnest expectation of the creature waiteth for the manifestation of the sons of God. For the creature was made subject to vanity, not willingly, but by reason of him who hath subjected the same in hope, because the creature itself also shall be delivered from bondage of corruption into the glorious liberty of the children of God. For we know that the whole creation groaneth and travaileth in pain together until now"* (Romans 8:18–22, KJV, emphasis added).

Animals suffered because of our sin. You see, we have free will. We can choose to follow God or not. That's our choice. Now we have to go back to Adam and Eve in the Garden of Eden. They chose to disobey God. Their action alienated them from God and was the downfall of all creation. Animals, on the other hand, have not lost their connection with God. They don't have free will to choose to worship God or not; they automatically worship Him. Animals have only one God. They don't make up other things to worship. They know their Maker and worship Him only. When He talks to them, they listen and obey. Humans, as we have seen, don't necessarily obey God's call. The sad thing is that animals have suffered because of our sin and disobedience. Animals didn't sin; they didn't disobey God; but because of the disobedience of man and woman, animals also suffered the penalty and were kicked out of the Garden of Eden. In God's plan of redemption, Jesus paid the ultimate price not only for us but for animals and all creation, for it says "the creature itself also shall be delivered from the bondage of corruption into the glorious liberty of the children of God." Let us keep our ears open to the message.

> Therefore if any man be in Christ, he is a new creature: old things are passed away; behold, all things are become new. And *all things are of God, who hath reconciled us to himself by Jesus Christ,* and hath given to us the ministry of reconciliation; to wit, that *God was in Christ, reconciling the world unto himself,* not imputing their trespasses unto them; and hath committed unto us the word of reconciliation. Now then we are embassadors for Christ, as though God beseech you by us: We pray you in Christ's stead, be ye reconciled to God. For he hath made him to be sin for us, who knew no sin; that we might be made the righteousness of God in him. (2 Corinthians 5:17–21, KJV, emphasis added)

Let's look closely: "all things are of God, who hath reconciled us to himself by Jesus Christ," and "God was in Christ, reconciling the world unto himself." What Jesus did for us, He did for the entire creation.

> Who is the image of the invisible God, the first born of every creature: *For by him were all things created, that are in heaven, and that are in earth, visible and invisible,* whether they be thrones, or dominions, or principalities, or powers: *all things were created by him, and for him: And he is before all things, and by him all things consist.* And he is the beginning, the first born from the dead; that *in all things he might have the preeminence. For it pleased the*

Father that in him should all fullness dwell; And, having made peace through the blood of his cross, by him to reconcile all things unto himself; by him, I say, whether they be things in earth, or things in heaven. And you that were sometime alienated and enemies in your mind by wicked works, yet now hath he reconciled in the body of his flesh through death, to present you holy and unblameable and unreprovable in his sight: If ye continue in the faith grounded and settled, and be not moved away from the hope of the gospel, which ye have heard, and which was preached to every creature which is under heaven; whereof I Paul am made a minister. (Colossians 1:15–23, KJV, emphasis added)

Again, look at what the apostle Paul wrote. He repeats himself to make sure it is very clear. God reconciled all things to Himself. All means all. All things were created by Him and for Him. He reconciled all things unto Himself.

"Of his own will begat he us with the word of truth, that we should be a kind of first fruits of his creatures" (James 1:18, KJV). Remember, we humans were made in the image of God. We were made to be caretakers of God's creation. I believe James is calling us to rise up and be what God intended us to be and put an end to our destructive nature.

All creatures were created by God for His pleasure. Jesus came to earth to fulfill the law of the old covenant and to make a new and better way. He allowed Himself to be sacrificed not only for humans but for all of His creatures and creation itself. God is very clear in His message. For humans to think that they are the only creatures that will enter heaven is extremely selfish, self-centered, and egotistical. God is a much bigger God than that. He didn't spend all of His creative talent making all of

His beautiful creatures to let them just be destroyed forever. He made them for a reason and for His pleasure.

"O the depth of the riches both of the wisdom and knowledge of God! how unsearchable are his judgments, and his ways past finding out! For who hath known the mind of the Lord? or who hath been his counsellor? Or who hath first given to him, and it shall be recompensed unto him again? For of him, and through him, and to him, are all things to whom be glory for ever. Amen" (Romans 11:33–36, KJV).

God is complete. When He does something, He does it completely. Jesus is the bridge to eternal life. This bridge is for all creatures, creation, and all of us humans. It's a free gift; all we have to do is accept it. Let us move forward to the other side of the bridge and get a glimpse of heaven and the fulfillment of God's promises.

The Rainbow Bridge

This book would not be complete without a copy of "The Rainbow Bridge."
Since we are now at the point in our journey to catch a glimpse of heaven,
this seemed the most appropriate place to include it. Countless veterinarian
facilities share a copy with grieving pet owners following a loss in hopes of
offering some sort of comfort during the family's time of need. Although it
is widely known and used, I could never find out who the author was. The
one thing that is for certain is that the author obviously knew what he or
she was talking about.

There is a bridge connecting heaven and earth. It is called
the Rainbow Bridge because of its many colors. Just this
side of the Rainbow Bridge is a land of lush meadows, gentle
hills, and cool valleys of sweet green grass and shade.

When a beloved pet dies, they go to this place. There is always
food, water, and warm spring weather. In this place old and
frail animals are young again. The sick are made well and the
maimed are made whole. They play all day with each other.

There is only one thing missing . . . . you! They are not with
their special person who loved them on earth. So, day after

day they run and play and wait until each, in their own time, suddenly stops, looks up, twitches their nose, perks their ears and excitedly stares beyond the others with overwhelming love. With barks of resounding joy they run from the group!

When you and special friend meet, you take him or her in your arms and lovingly embrace them for all the lost years. Your face is kissed again and again and again as you look once more into the eyes of your trusting pet. Then, together you cross the Rainbow Bridge, never to be separated again.[12]

---

[12]   Jack Canfield et al., *Chicken Soup for the Pet Lover's Soul* (Dearfield Beach: Health Communications, Inc., 1998) 323-324

A Glimpse of Heaven

I received this e-mail some time back. I have no idea who the author is. That seems to happen a lot with these things. It's one of those mysterious e-mails that are forwarded on without any idea of their origin. I guess it is just one of those mysteries of the Internet. Anyway, I thought the message was interesting and was an appropriate way to start off this chapter, especially following "The Rainbow Bridge." It is about a man and his dog:

> A man and his dog were walking along a road. The man was enjoying the scenery when it suddenly occurred to him that he was dead. He remembered dying and that the dog walking beside him had been dead for years. He wondered where the road was leading them. After a while, they came to a high, white stone wall along one side of the road. It looked like fine marble.

> At the top of a long hill, it was broken by a tall arch that glowed in the sunlight.

> When he was standing before it, he saw a magnificent gate in the arch that looked like mother-of-pearl, and the street that led to the gate looked like pure gold. He and the dog walked

toward the gate, and as he got closer, he saw a man at a desk to one side. When he was close enough, he called out, "Excuse me, where are we?"

"This is heaven, sir," the man answered.

"Wow! Would you happen to have some water?" the man asked.

"Of course, sir. Come right in, and I'll have some ice water brought right up."

The man gestured, and the gate began to open.

"Can my friend come in too?" the traveler asked, gesturing toward his dog.

"I'm sorry, sir, but we don't accept pets."

The man thought a moment and then turned back toward the road and continued the way he had been going with his dog. After another long walk and at the top of another long hill, he came to a dirt road leading through a farm gate that looked as if it had never been closed. There was no fence. As he approached the gate, he saw a man inside leaning against a tree and reading a book.

"Excuse me!" he called to the man. "Do you have any water?"

"Yeah, sure, there's a pump over there. Come on in."

"How about my friend here?" The traveler gestured to the dog.

"There should be a bowl by the pump."

They went through the gate, and sure enough, there was an old-fashioned hand pump with a bowl beside it. The traveler filled the water bowl and took a long drink himself. Then he gave some to the dog. When they were full, he and the dog walked back toward the man who was standing by the tree.

"What do you call this place?" the traveler asked.

"This is heaven," he answered.

"Well, that's confusing," the traveler said. "The man down the road said that was heaven too."

"Oh, you mean the place with the gold street and pearly gates? Nope. That's hell."

"Doesn't it make you mad for them to use your name like that?"

"No, we're just happy that they screen out the folks who would leave their best friends behind."

I really like that story. All of us who love animals and have lost one of our dear pets want to know that we will be reunited with our best friends in heaven. That was the whole reason I started off on this quest for the truth so long ago. Granted, I have learned so much more than I ever imagined along the way, but this was the destination I was longing to reach. I must be a very slow traveler. You know how I have said that when God tells you to do something, it is important that you do it? I have shared that I am quite the procrastinator; I get off track easily and then second-guess what I am supposed to do, which ends up with me just stuck in the mud not moving anywhere. During one of those off-track, stuck-in-the-mud times, Darlene, a dear, sweet lady at my church, brought an article for me to read. It was from the February 2005 edition of *Guideposts*. The article was titled "Do Pets Go to Heaven?" and it was written by Ptolemy Tompkins, Senior Editor. When I received that article, I knew God was using Darlene to help get my feet out of the mud and continue on the project He wanted me to finish. With that in mind, let's move forward and see what we can see.

This has been a long journey to get to this place and see a glimpse of heaven. Can you even imagine what heaven is going to be like? Sometimes I just sit and ponder about heaven, trying to visualize what it will look like. I know that if the truth be told, most of us have had doubts about heaven's existence. We may believe in God and say we believe in the Bible, but heaven is this unknown entity. Do we really know that it exists? Could it be that when we die, there is no more— that we just cease to exist? When you've lost a loved one, whether a person or a pet, those nagging doubts haunt you. It is about believing in something you cannot see. It is about having blind faith. And the bottom line is having faith can be tough, especially during the dark times in life. But what I have found is that it is this faith—faith that what you cannot see is real—that gets you through the darkest of times.

"For we are saved by hope: but hope that is seen is not hope: for what a man seeth, why doth he yet hope for? But if we hope for that we see not, then do we with patience wait for it" (Romans 8:24–25, KJV). "Now faith is the substance of things hoped for, the evidence of things not seen" (Hebrews 11:1, KJV).

I remember my mom saying that if we didn't believe, there would be no reason to go on. There is a great truth in that. There would be no sense of any kind of order or purpose. There would seem to be no meaning to life and our existence. Life would seem too unbearable.

Ptolemy Tompkins shared in his article, "Do Pets Go to Heaven?" his own journey to find out if there is a place in heaven for animals. Being an animal lover and losing his beloved rabbit, he had a personal interest. He quoted many scriptures in his article that I have already shared with you in previous chapters, such as the covenant God made with Noah and all the animals, and the statement that "all flesh shall see the salvation of God" (Luke 3:6). He also quoted the scripture that was a favorite passage of St. Francis of Assisi, Mark 16:15, in which Jesus commanded his disciples, "Go ye into all the world, and preach the gospel to every creature.[13]"

I have heard that when someone is terminally ill and approaching death, it seems the walls between this world and heaven become very thin. I have read and heard firsthand accounts of people witnessing this. The person who is approaching death starts seeing loved ones that have died years before, as if they are coming to usher them into heaven. My dear friend who got me started on this quest told me about what she experienced when her brother was close to death. He was in the hospital with not much time left. She stated that he looked like he could see something and started reaching out to it. It caught her off guard, and she didn't know what he was doing. Shortly afterward, he died. When thinking back on that moment, she wondered if he was seeing one of their family members who had died years before, but he was reaching down low, not higher where they would have been standing if, in fact, they were there. Then she realized he was probably reaching out to their dogs that had died in the house fire years back.

Another story I heard came from one of the vet techs at the animal clinic. She had Clifford the Big Red Dog, as she called him, whom she

---

[13]   Ptolemy Tompkins, "Do Pets Go to Heaven?" *Guideposts* (February 2005):86-92.

loved very much. When her father became terminally ill with cancer, he and her mom came to live with her and her family so she could care for them. Clifford and her father became very close and bonded deeply. The dog would take naps and sleep with her father. He never seemed to leave his side. Tabitha, the vet tech, shared that she always knew what kind of day her father had based on how Clifford acted. If Clifford was happy and greeted her, she knew her dad had a good day. If Clifford didn't come to greet her when she came home, she knew her dad didn't have such a good day and Clifford would be right by his side. As the story goes, Clifford the Big Red Dog became ill, coincidentally with cancer, and died in September. When her father's illness became worse and he was approaching death, he would talk about that dog always being right by him and never leaving his side. Her father would talk to him and appeared to be stroking his coat while he told him how much he loved him. Her dad would say, "This dog loves me so much, he won't leave me alone." Could it be that Clifford the Big Red Dog came to be with him to escort him into the next life? Her father died shortly afterward in April of the following year. She believes Clifford was there to comfort her dad and walk with him along their journey to heaven.

We may never know for certain what heaven will exactly be like until we get there (it isn't like we can plan to go there for a summer vacation, although I wish we could), but we can get a glimpse of it from what God has revealed in the Bible. God wants us to trust Him. He has given us multiple images of what heaven is going to be like and who all will be there. Let us reflect on God's promise of the covenant to come that God will make with man and all creation. We will begin with a look at the peaceable kingdom revealed in Isaiah 11. This is one of the main scriptures that Ptolemy Tompkins shared that gave him great comfort that his beloved pets would be in heaven and is one that I hold very close to my heart. We will look at several other scriptures that share about God's plan and heaven. I encourage you, while you are reading these scriptures, to take time to truly meditate and ponder what God is sharing. Open up your heart and your mind to visualize really what heaven is like. I believe you will be truly comforted by what you start to see.

> The wolf will live with the lamb, the leopard will lie down with the goat, the calf and the lion and the yearling together; and a little child will lead them, the cow will feed with the bear, their young will lie down together, and the lion will eat straw like the ox. The infant will play near the hole of the cobra, and the young child put his hand into the viper's nest. They will neither harm nor destroy on all my holy mountain, for the earth will be full of the knowledge of the Lord as the waters cover the sea. (Isaiah 11:6–9, NIV)

"And in that day will I make a covenant for them with the beasts of the field and with the fowls of heaven, and with the creeping things of the ground: and I will break the bow and the sword and the battle out of the earth, and will make them to lie down safely" (Hosea 2:18, KJV).

"The wolf and the lamb shall feed together and the lion shall eat straw like the bullock: and dust shall be the serpent's meat. They shall not hurt nor destroy in all my holy mountain, saith the Lord" (Isaiah 65:25, KJV).

"Remember ye not the former things, neither consider the things of old. Behold, I will do a new thing, now it shall spring forth; shall ye not know it? I will even make a way in the wilderness, and rivers in the desert. The beast of the field shall honour me, the dragons and the owls: because I give waters in the wilderness, and rivers in the desert to give drink to my people, my chosen" (Isaiah 43:18–20, KJV).

"Lift up your eyes to the heavens and look upon the earth beneath: for the heavens shall vanish away like smoke, and the earth shall wax old like a garment and they that dwell therein shall die in like manner: but my salvation shall be forever, and my righteousness shall not be abolished" (Isaiah 51:6, KJV).

"For, behold, I create new heavens and a new earth: and the former shall not be remembered, nor come into mind" (Isaiah 65:17, KJV).

"And it shall come to pass, that from one new moon to another, and from one sabbath to another, shall all flesh come to worship before me, saith the Lord" (Isaiah 66:23, KJV).

Remember, Jesus made the new covenant. The old covenant has passed away, and He made a new and better one that will be everlasting. Although God's plan in the Garden of Eden went amiss with the fall of mankind, God's ways are far above our ways, and His plan will come full circle to what He originally intended. That is what heaven is all about.

Let's look at what the apostle Paul reveals about heaven. Paul shared about an experience he had that sounds very similar to a kind of near-death or out-of-body experience. He was overwhelmed by what he had encountered. He was so awestruck by the wonders he saw that words failed to describe the magnitude of the beauty. We can learn a lot about heaven from those who have experienced a little more than a glimpse of it.

> I know a man in Christ who fourteen years ago was caught up to the third heaven. Whether it was in the body or out of the body I do not know—God knows. And I know that this man—whether in the body or apart from the body I do not know, but God knows—was caught up to paradise. He heard

inexpressible things, things that man is not permitted to tell. I will boast about a man like that, but I will not boast about myself, except about my weaknesses. Even if I should choose to boast, I would not be a fool, because I would be speaking the truth. But I refrain, so no one will think more of me than is warranted by what I do or say. (2 Corinthians 12:2–6, NIV)

What the apostle Paul experienced was indescribable and extremely wonderful. It was an experience he never forgot. Paul experienced heaven firsthand and was able to come back to tell about it. He had no doubt that heaven was a real place. In knowing that, we can find hope. Paul also sheds light on how it will be different from here on earth, such as regarding our bodies.

But some man will say, How are the dead raised up? And with what body do they come? Thou fool, that which thou sowest is not quickened, except it die: And that which thou sowest, thou sowest not that body that shall be, but bare grain, it may chance of wheat, or of some other grain: But God giveth it a body as it hath pleased him, and to every seed his own body. All flesh is not the same flesh: but there is one kind of flesh of beasts, another of fishes, and another of birds. There are also celestial bodies, and bodies terrestrial: but the glory of the celestial bodies is one, and the glory of the terrestrial is another. There is one glory of the sun, and another glory of the moon, and another glory of the stars: for one star differeth from another star in glory. So also is the resurrection of the dead. It is sown in corruption; it is raised in incorruption: It is sown in dishonor; it is raised in glory: it is sown in weakness; it is raised in power: It is sown a natural body; it is raised a spiritual body. There is a natural body, and there is a spiritual body (1 Corinthians 15:35–44, KJV).

"Therefore we are always confident, knowing that, whilst we are at home in the body, we are absent from the Lord: (For we walk by faith, not by sight:) We are confident, I say, and willing rather to be absent from the body, and to be present with the Lord" (2 Corinthians 5:6–8, KJV).

God has revealed His plan of the new covenant to the prophets. This plan clearly shared about animals and humans living in peace together. Jesus came and made the new covenant and eternal bridge to heaven. Paul had a glimpse of heaven, which was too profound and overwhelming for him even to speak clearly about. He shared about how we all will be transformed and changed.

Let's move on to the book of Revelation. This book was written by the apostle John when he was on the island of Patmos as a result of a revelation he received from Jesus Christ. Again, like Paul's encounter, this sounds very similar to some sort of near death or out of body experience. Jesus comes to John in a vision and shows him of things to come: "After this I looked, and, behold, a door was opened in heaven: and the first voice which I heard was as it were of a trumpet talking with me; which said, Come up hither, and I will shew thee things which must be hereafter. And immediately I was in the spirit: and, behold, a throne was set in heaven, and one sat on the throne. And he that sat was to look upon like a jasper and a sardine stone: and there was a rainbow round about the throne, in sight like unto an emerald." (Revelation 4:1–3, KJV)

In this vision, John sees what heaven is like:

> And before the throne there was a sea of glass like unto crystal: and in the midst of the throne, and round about the throne, were four beasts full of eyes before and behind. And the first beast was like a lion, and the second beast like a calf, and the

third beast had a face as a man, and the fourth beast was like a flying eagle. And the four beasts had each of them six wings about him; and they were full of eyes within: and they rest not day and night, saying, Holy, holy, holy, Lord God Almighty, which was, and is, and is to come. And when those beasts give glory and honour and thanks to him that sat on the throne, who liveth for ever and ever, The four and twenty elders fall down before him that sat on the throne, and worship him that liveth for ever and ever, and cast their crowns before the throne, saying, Thou art worthy, O Lord, to receive glory and honour and power: for thou hast created all things, and for thy pleasure they are and were created. (Revelation 4:6–11, KJV)

"And every creature which is in heaven, and on the earth, and under the earth, and such as are in the sea, and all that are in them, heard I saying, Blessing, and honour, and glory, and power, be unto him that sitteth upon the throne, and unto the Lamb for ever and ever" (Revelation 5:13, KJV).

"And I saw a new heaven and a new earth: for the first heaven and the first earth were passed away; and there was no more sea" (Revelation 21:1, KJV).

"And God shall wipe away all tears from their eyes; and there shall be no more death, neither sorrow, nor crying, neither shall there be any more pain: for the former things passed away. And he that sat upon the throne said, Behold, I make all things new. And he said unto me, Write: for these words are true and faithful" (Revelation 21:4–5, KJV).

"And the city had no need of the sun, neither of the moon, to shine in it: for the glory of God did lighten it, and the Lamb is the light thereof" (Revelation 21:23, KJV).

God plans to make everything new. There will be no more pain or sorrow. All will worship God, including all creatures. All things will be as originally intended. These are only a few scriptures that I found that helped describe heaven. We could keep digging and find even more. The main point from the scriptures is that it is very clear that animals will be there. God has an interest in all of his creation and wants to save all things. To borrow a phrase from C. S. Lewis, we have been living in the shadow lands. What we see here is only a shadow of what things will be in heaven. It is as if we are living in a dark room. We can see, because our eyes become adjusted to the dark, but we can't see the true essence of things or the true colors—only a diluted, cloudy image. If we can turn the lights on in the room, we can then see things more clearly. Heaven is the true creation: vibrant, alive, and filled with God's love and wisdom. God had to make a way for this reality that we live in to fade away and for all of us to experience His true creation in its full splendor. Heaven is about God's perfect place. It will be a beauty that goes beyond what our words can say. There will be no more pain and sickness. There will be no more tears. And quite honestly, it wouldn't be perfect if animals and our furry best friends weren't there.

So our journey has come full circle. We have arrived at our destination. We can rest assured that all of our animals will indeed be in heaven to greet us and be with us for eternity. The rainbow bridge is a reality. The message has been there all along hidden within God's word. It is sad that some people have put up blinders to this very real and true fact. But for us, we now know the truth, know that our God is very real, amazingly loving and compassionate, and has everything under control regarding His plan for all of us and all of His creation. We can sleep easy at night and have no more worries or doubts about our critters' fate. We do indeed know the truth. In spite of all the perils, wickedness, lies, and deceit in the world, we no longer have to succumb to them. The truth has set us free. We now know beyond a shadow of a doubt that when we enter heaven, all of our little furry and feathery babies will be waiting together to greet us, to love on us, and to give us lots and lots of kisses. We will all be able to live happily ever after together forever in heaven.

> For my thoughts are not your thoughts, neither are your ways my ways, saith the Lord. For as the heavens are higher than the earth, so are my ways higher than your ways, and my thoughts than your thoughts. For as the rain cometh down, and the snow from heaven, and returneth not thither, but watereth the earth, and maketh it bring forth and bud, that it may give seed to the sower, and bread to the eater: So shall my word be that goeth forth out of my mouth: it shall not return unto me void, but it shall accomplish that which I please, and it shall prosper in the thing whereto I sent it. For ye shall go out with joy, and be led forth with peace: the mountains and the hills shall break forth before you into singing, and all the trees of the field shall clap their hands. Instead of the thorn shall come up the fir tree, and instead of the briar shall come up the myrtle tree: and it shall be to the Lord for a name, for an everlasting sign that shall not be cut off. (Isaiah 55:8–13, KJV)

A Word on Vegetarianism

As you probably have figured out by now, I have a strong love for God's creatures. That is just the way God made me. My best friends have always been animals. They seem to know more about what it takes to be a true and faithful friend. I was raised, as probably most of us were, in a meat-eating family. Although I ate meat, I never believed in hunting or hurting animals in any way. I could never understand how someone could go out and kill an innocent, beautiful creature, let alone enjoy the killing process! It repulsed me. As I grew older, I started to realize that my behavior was incongruent with the values I held.

I believe now that God had a plan for me all along, because I truly believe that He was talking to me long ago when He instilled an awful, overwhelming guilt inside of me regarding my actions. How could I justify eating a steak or a juicy cheeseburger when I couldn't bear the thought of hurting, yet alone killing, a beautiful, innocent cow with those big, loving brown eyes? I had to make some important changes in my life. My behavior needed to change to become more congruent with my values. It was at that time I made a decision to become vegetarian and no longer be a flesh eater. Needless to say, my family thought I was quite weird and ridiculous. I had to stand strong, alone, determined and do what I thought was right. At first it was hard. Family gatherings were very awkward. Many people (including family) didn't like the changes in me. I was different and no longer conformed to the customs that I used to conform to. I made choices in my life to make my behavior more congruent with my values. That was my choice to do that. Everyone has to be accountable for the choices they make. No one else can do it for them.

Through this journey of mine I have had many questions surface about what God really thinks on this matter. God answered the questions I had. As we have already covered, God's plan was for all creation to be vegetarian. In the first chapter of Genesis, God shares this plan: "And God said, Behold, I have given you every herb bearing seed, which is upon the face of all the earth, and every tree, in the which is the fruit of a tree yielding seed; to you it shall be for meat. And to every beast of the earth, and to every fowl of the air, and to every thing that creepeth upon the earth, wherein there is life, I have given every green herb for meat: and it was so" (Genesis 1:29–30, KJV).

He made all animals, all creatures, and human beings to eat fruits, vegetables, and herbs. It was to be meat, or food, for us all. This was God's plan. "And God saw every thing that he had made, and, behold, it was very good" (Genesis 1:31, KJV).

Man and woman's job was to care for the land and take care of all God's creatures. All were supposed to live in peace. Now we know that didn't last. Adam and Eve were kicked out of the Garden of Eden. The land was cursed because of their sin. Man and woman still did not eat flesh until after the great flood. I know many people use this to justify their flesh-eating habits, because when Noah, his family, and all the creatures were able to leave the ark, God said, "And the fear of you and the dread of you shall be upon every beast of the earth, and upon every fowl of the air, upon all that moveth upon the earth, and upon all the fishes of the sea; into your hand are they delivered. Every moving thing that liveth shall be meat for you; even as the green herbs have I given you all things" (Genesis 9:2–3, KJV).

Now, I want you to take a moment and ponder this. The entire earth had been flooded. This was not just an ordinary flood but a devastating flood that covered the entire earth! All living creatures died that were not on the ark. All vegetation would have died or would have been severely damaged. The food supply on the ark had to have been dwindling down. God allowed Noah and his family to eat flesh along with the greens of the land when they came back into existence. Do you really think He wanted flesh to be humans' main source of food? I think not. I really believe He wanted it to be temporary, but you know how humans are. They want more than enough.

Let's look at a couple of other scriptures that may shed light on God's desire. In the book of Leviticus, God instructs that the land needs a Sabbath year of rest. He will provide food for everyone during that year of rest: "And the sabbath of the land shall be meat for you; for thee, and for thy servant, and for thy maid, and for thy hired servant, and for thy stranger that sojourneth with thee, and for thy cattle, and for the beast that are in thy land, shall all the increase there of be meat" (Leviticus 25:6–7, KJV). Remember, *meat* means "food." God is talking about how the vegetation of the land will be food for all including the animals.

The book of Proverbs has a couple of very interesting scriptures that deserve to be looked at: "The lambs are for clothing, and the goats are the price of the field. And thou shalt have goats' milk enough for thy food, for the food of thy household, and for the maintenance for thy maidens" (Proverbs 27:26–27, KJV). "He that tilleth his land shall have plenty of bread: but he that followeth after vain person shall have poverty enough" (Proverbs 28:19, KJV). Both of these scriptures show that food comes from the land, or milk, but not from flesh. No animals need to die for us to have nourishment.

I want to share a scripture I found in the book of Isaiah that I found significant: "Come now, and let us reason together, saith the Lord: though your sins be as scarlet, they shall be as white as snow, though they be red like crimson, they shall be as wool. If ye be willing and obedient, ye shall *eat the good of the land:* But if ye refuse and rebel, ye shall be devoured with the sword: for the mouth of the Lord hath spoken it" (Isaiah 1:18–20, KJV, emphasis added). Again, God is saying we can "eat the good of the land." I don't get any indication that He is saying, "slaughter and eat all the flesh of the animals you want."

Let us move ahead and look at the time Jesus walked on this earth. God came down to earth in flesh form to show us the way. Jesus spent forty days and forty nights in the wilderness and was tempted by Satan. Jesus fasted during this entire time. I am sure He must have been starving. Satan knew this too. You know that if Satan was going to tempt Jesus, he was going to go for what Jesus would really want. He wasn't going to tempt Him with something that would be easy to say no to. He was going to go for what Jesus would really be craving.

"And when the tempter came to him, he said, If thou be the Son of God, command that these stones be made bread. But he answered and said, It is written, Man shall not live by bread alone, but by every word that proceedeth out of the mouth of God" (Matthew 4:3–4, KJV).

Bread is what Jesus was craving! He didn't want a KC strip steak, juicy cheeseburger, or any other slab of flesh. His favorite food was bread! If that doesn't say something about the heart of God, I don't know what does.

As I said earlier, everyone has to make their own choices and has to be accountable for the choices they make. Every action, every decision we make has an effect on others, whether it be good or bad. God has allowed humans to eat animals' flesh. Does He like us slaughtering animals and overindulging in eating their flesh? I am sure He does not. But let's be real—we do many things that He does not like. Do we change our ways to be more like Christ? If we are truly honest, the answer is no. I was listening to a preacher on a Christian radio station talk about God's feeling about divorce. God doesn't like divorce. He wants marriages to last. That was his original plan. But because of how humans are, He has allowed divorce. Moses made laws on divorce and how to go about it. This doesn't mean God is happy with divorce. It just means He has allowed it to take place. Isn't it the same with eating flesh? All I can say is that I know God has put it on my heart to not eat flesh and to honor His creatures. As for me and my house, we will serve the Lord. This is one of the choices I have made to serve Him. You have to make your own choice.

One last note that I have to include is about what it will be like in heaven for eternity. Let's revisit a couple of scriptures in the book of Isaiah:

> The wolf also shall dwell with the lamb, and the leopard shall lie down with the kid; and the calf and the young lion and the fatling together: and a little child shall lead them. And the cow and the bear shall feed; their young ones shall lie down together: and the lion shall eat straw like the ox. And the sucking child shall play on the hole of the asp, and the weaned child shall put his

hand on the cockatrice den. They shall not hurt nor destroy in all my holy mountain: for the earth shall be full of the knowledge of the Lord, as the waters cover the sea. (Isaiah 11:6–9, KJV)

Remember, this is repeated again in chapter 65 of Isaiah: "The wolf and the lamb shall feed together, and the lion shall eat straw like the bullock: and dust shall be the serpent's meat. They shall not hurt nor destroy in all my holy mountain, saith the Lord" (Isaiah 65:25, KJV).

Both of these scriptures show that animals will be vegetarian again. Also, no one will "hurt nor destroy," which indicates that there won't be any killing. Let's look at the book of Revelation:

"And God shall wipe away all tears from their eyes: and there shall be no more death, neither sorrow, nor crying, neither shall there be any more pain: for the former things are passed away. And he that sat upon the throne said, Behold, I make all things new. And he said unto me, write: for these words are true and faithful" (Revelation 21:4–5, KJV).

There will be no more pain, no more sorrow, and no more killing. I could go on and on with other scriptures, but at this point I don't want to be too redundant. What God did in the beginning with the Garden of Eden will be in the end. Everything will come full circle. All will eat fruit, veggies, and herbs. Humans and animals will live in peace together just as it was always meant to be.

So for those hunters out there, when you die, don't plan on taking your gun or bow and arrow, because in heaven, you won't be allowed to use them! And the big secret is you won't even want to!

Animals Have Feelings Too!

photo taken by Suzy Mast-Lee

I have debated whether to include this chapter or not. After thoughtful consideration, I decided that I wouldn't be doing a thorough job for God if I didn't. I know for most of you reading this, what I am about to say you already know. You wouldn't be reading this book if you didn't have a strong love for animals. This will be a confirmation of your own knowledge and experiences. For others, it might encourage you to look at animals in a bit different light. This chapter will hopefully nudge you to broaden your view of the nature of animals. Being a clinical social worker working with children, youth, and families for more than twenty years and being an animal lover for longer, I have noticed striking similarities in our psychosocial development. Animals really are no different from us humans. All of God's creatures have the inherent need for food, water, shelter, and safety. Those needs have to be met in order to sustain life. Humans and creatures are all the same on that issue. If any of us go without those needs being met for an extended period of time, we will perish in one way or another. I want to go further, though, and show how the needs for belonging, love, and social interaction are just as crucial to all creatures' survival. The bottom line is that God gave all of His creatures emotions. We are well aware that human beings have a wide range of feelings. Sometimes we are less likely to consider that other creatures possess a similar array of emotions.

Let's first explore how each creature has his or her own personality. To better discuss this, let me share a few personal examples that I have at home. All I have to do is look at my different pets to experience how each one is different from the others. Their little personalities shine through. For example, Noah, my buff cocker spaniel, has such a sweet disposition. He never holds a grudge. He is extremely bonded to me and loves to show affection. He is always the gentleman and waits for me wherever we go. Noah also has revealed his own unique nature by his strong passion for tomatoes. He absolutely loves them. I plant tomato plants every summer. Noah's first summer with me, he became interested in the tomatoes growing in the garden. He picked one and ate it all. Thus his passion grew from there. He guards his tomato plants every summer and waits with anticipation for the tomatoes to grow and ripen. As soon as he spots a red one, he picks it and eats it. I have to watch him so he doesn't eat them all! Noah sometimes becomes impatient and picks one that is still green. He will eat it, but it is obvious he doesn't like the taste quite as well as the ruby-red ones. Noah is definitely a connoisseur of tomatoes! Jonah, my tricolor cocker spaniel, has his own ways. Although he has become quite the little lover boy and is extremely sensitive to everything, especially the spiritual realm, he can have his temperamental moments. He is the one who gets irritated the easiest. If he is tired, it is best to let him sleep, because he can be extremely cranky. He always wants to be first at everything. If Jonah is scared, he will seek me out, identifying me as his protector. Hannah, on the other hand, is my floozy girl. She loves to be the center of attention and especially loves to be the center of attention with all the boys. She has an extremely contrary nature and can be a picky eater. When Luke came to me, he was very timid. I think a lot of that was a result of the life he had prior to coming to Funky Farm, which consisted of abuse and neglect. He doesn't like to get into trouble and is very eager to please. Luke loves to be under the blankets. Honestly, I had never known a dog who likes to be totally covered up with a blanket (including his head) until I met Luke.

Thumper and Pete, my cottontail rabbits that I took in as orphan babies, had their own personalities and dispositions. Thumper definitely had a bold personality. She seemed to have no fear of anything. She was always looking for an adventure. Thumper would plot and figure out how to get behind furniture and into things she wasn't supposed to. I always had to watch out for her and what she was getting herself into. Pete, on the other hand, was more laid back and easy going. I'll never forget the time I realized that she had a special music preference. On Saturdays I have the TV on PBS to listen to all the how-to shows while I am taking care of chores around the house. At 5:00 p.m., *The Lawrence*

Welk Show comes on. Pete would come in the family room and lie down sprawled out in front of the television set. She repeated this almost every Saturday when that show came on. I'm not saying I share her taste in music, but she definitely seemed to enjoy listening to the music on the show. Speaking of music preferences, I have to tell you about my albino parakeets I had while I was in college. Ralph and Charli would travel with me on trips back home for the weekend. I would have music playing during these car rides. The birds usually remained fairly quiet while the music played except when it was the Beatles or Billy Joel. When I put on the Beatles or Billy Joel, Ralph would sing along. He definitely enjoyed their music.

Everyone has his or her own personality and disposition. Animals are no different. If you have human children, you see the same thing. No two of your kids are alike. Each one has different interests and preferences. Each one has his or her own unique way of doing things. Animals are the same way. When God breathed the breath of life into every human and every living creature, they all became living souls. But this isn't to say that all have a generic sort of living soul, so that all humans are the same or all animals are all the same. God isn't into mass production. God is an artist. Everything He makes is a masterpiece, one of a kind, an original. When God breathes the breath of life into each person and each creature, there is something special and unique He breathes into each one. Everyone who has pets knows that each one of your babies is different in its own special way. That is what God breathed into them.

Now we really need to address the effects of abuse and neglect. Abuse and neglect rob a creature of one or more of their basic needs for survival (food, water, shelter, and safety). Chronic abuse can be tragically traumatizing. Being a social worker, I have seen the crushing and sometimes debilitating effects on children and teens who were victims of abuse. Physically they may heal, but the emotional scars can last a lifetime. Abuse and neglect affect animals the same way. If an animal has been a victim of severe abuse or neglect, the awful trauma will affect how they view their world and surroundings. The world will seem to be an unsafe place. Trust has been thwarted. Depending on the nature of the abuse, the creature may see humans as unsafe, other animals as unsafe, or both. Just like humans, their response is to go into a fight-or-flight-or-freeze mode. Behaviors that may be exhibited include anger and aggression, extreme timidity and fear, and possible unusual behaviors when in trigger situations or when around a trigger object. Trigger situations and objects are situations or objects that may be similar to something that has caused pain in the past. An association is made between the object or situation and the abuse, usually unconsciously. These responses may seem extremely irrational, but our emotions aren't always rational.

Let me give you a few examples that I have witnessed. Albert, my cocker spaniel (who is in heaven now), came to me from someone who knew someone who was breeding cockers. Albert was one of the cockers who hadn't found a home. They were going take him to the pound because he was five months old and wouldn't be sellable. I bought him for twenty dollars. I quickly found out that he obviously hadn't been treated well. He exhibited very odd behaviors. When it was feeding time, he would guard his food and would almost hoard it. If he was ever around a woman with dark hair, he would become extremely agitated. It didn't transfer to men with dark hair—only women. On a hunch, I wanted to find out what color of hair the woman had who was breeding the cockers. It was confirmed that she, indeed, had dark hair. Something awful must have happened to Albert while he was there. There apparently were a lot of dogs, and there must not have been a lot of food to go around.

I never found out exactly what had happened to Albert, but I was left with dealing with the aftereffects. With time, patience, and a lot of love, Albert's bizarre ways slowly diminished. Eventually (after a few years), women with dark hair didn't bother him anymore.

I adopted Boxwood, a rabbit, from an animal clinic. He apparently had been brought to a shelter with a broken back leg. Apparently, someone threw him out of a car window while it was moving. The shelter immediately transferred him to the clinic for medical intervention. He was skin and bones. He was at the clinic for quite some time. They planned to have him return to the shelter once he had healed from his injuries. I met Boxwood during one of my trips to the clinic for another one of my rabbits, Clover, who was receiving treatment for an abscess. I heard his sad story. Due to my frequent visits to the clinic during that time, I saw Boxwood a lot. My heart melted, so I decided to adopt Boxwood. The vet told me that he had a cantankerous disposition. He would charge at anyone who invaded his space and bit many of the vet techs when they had to change his cage or check on his leg. The vet told me that Boxwood might always be this way because of his severe trauma that he endured and lack of trust. I adopted him anyway. After bringing him home, I encountered his charging and biting behavior. I didn't let it stop me from loving on him, praying for him, and speaking kind words with a soft, calm voice. He received care, love, and regular meals (something he hadn't had). God is a healing God. With time and consistent care, Boxwood learned to trust me. He no longer charges or bites. In fact, he is a real sweet guy. I know God called me to adopt him and provide a safe and nurturing environment for him. That is exactly what Boxwood needed.

You have already heard the story about Luke, my German short-haired pointer. The Animal Control lady told me that besides being severely neglected, he was also a victim of physical abuse. When I brought him home, it became very clear that someone had smacked him a lot. If anyone attempted to pet and touch his head, he would slump back as if afraid they would hit him. With God, love, patience, and consistency, Luke started to realize no one was going to harm him. He received regular meals and a constant water supply. Luke's trust level started to grow. Apparently there was another dog where he had lived that was allowed to pick on and fight Luke. When he came to me, he was extremely shy, timid, and kept a distance from my other dogs. I didn't even hear him bark for a long time. My other dogs were quite social and love to play. They have their own game of tag that they have developed. When they would play their games in the yard, Luke would stay away and keep to himself. It was as if he wasn't even interested in playing with them but content with being in his own little world. Cruelty and abuse create long-lasting scars on the victims. My dogs aren't allowed to pick on or fight with each other. Luke wasn't being threatened, but he still remained very cautious. My dogs treated Luke with love and compassion. With time, he became more curious about their games. He eventually started to participate and was greeted with enthusiasm and inclusion. Luke found his voice and a loving family. He now barks and plays just like the rest of them.

What can we learn from this? Abuse of any kind takes a toll on its victims, whether the victims are human or animals. If the victim remains in the deplorable, crippling situation, the victim can be crippled for life. With intervention, having basic needs met, experiencing love from others who can be trusted, and consistency, healing can take place. There is the hope.

The next issue we need to discuss is relationship development, starting with parenting. In many ways (not all) parenting animals is similar to parenting children. I have worked with children and families for more than half my life, and I have seen that there are basic ingredients that need to be in place to foster healthy psychosocial development. There has to be a trust that you will meet the child's needs (human or animal). I have to say here that I know some animals have more needs than others. For example, dogs require more than some other animals do, such as cats. Others may be far greater. Trust is established with consistency of your behavior. I can't stress this enough. Basic needs have to be met consistently and faithfully. It has to be like clockwork. They know you provide for them. This fosters trust and demonstrates to them that you are a safe person. You are a good, responsible caretaker, and isn't that what God has called us to be? And through building trust, establishing a consistent routine, and meeting their needs, it's important to develop and foster that relationship. Get to know your pet. Find out his or her likes and dislikes—what makes him or her tick. Show love and affection. Spend quality time together. Remember, God made every creature different and unique. There are no duplicates. Cherish those moments together. I have learned through my work and life that relationships are everything. They are what make life worth living. Relationships are the catalyst for change and can heal broken hearts. "Above all, love each other deeply, because love covers a multitude of sins" (1 Peter 4:8, NIV).

This leads me into another issue with parenting, which is discipline. I am not going to spend much time on this but want to point out something to think about. Let me share another example from my dog Albert. I have already shared about how he came to me with a previous history of neglect and abuse and issues related to that. When I was trying to house-train him, it became quite evident that what worked for Ashley, my other cocker, did not work for Albert. Ashley never wanted to be in trouble. Therefore, once I got her on a routine schedule of going outside and I was faithfully consistent with it, she was house-trained immediately. The problem was with me, not her. Once I committed to being faithfully consistent with taking her out on a regular schedule, there was no longer a problem. Consistency definitely helped Albert, but it wasn't enough. I hate to say I resorted to spankings when he had an accident in the house. It didn't make a difference. I tried putting him in a crate when I was gone. He made a mess in there. Negative consequences were no deterrent for him. Then I realized that he probably was used to negative consequences because of where he came from. I decided to go at it with a different strategy. I gave no response to the negative behavior but only praised the positive behavior. If he made a mess in the house, I gave no reaction. I took him outside, and when Albert pottied or pooped outside, I made a huge fuss about how he was such a good boy. I stayed consistent with this strategy. With a bit of time, it eventually worked! Albert decided he loved to be praised, and he stopped the negative behavior of making a mess in the house. What is the moral of the story? Just like with human kids, sometimes you have to change your strategy if it isn't working and try a different approach. Be consistent and give it some time. You'll find something that works. That's part of being a good parent. Not every discipline style works for every child, and that includes animals as well.

Create a safe environment. Your kids (humans and animals) need to see you as safe and know that home is safe. Teasing and any sort of mean behavior fosters insecurities. This can manifest itself in the child (human or animal) as either timid and anxious behavior or bullying and aggressive behavior. Either one is not healthy. Your mood is very important. Animals are sponges and are very in tune with your emotions and behavior. It is important to keep a calm and loving disposition (at least for the most part); otherwise we can easily move into the abusive mode that we have previously talked about. They need to see you as in charge of your emotions instead of your emotions being in charge of you.

Animals develop and need relationships just like humans. That is the way God made us—all of us. Just like children need to learn from adults and other children about right and wrong, social etiquette, limit setting, problem solving, playing, and such, animals need to learn from others as well. Animals need to be around others of their own kind to learn social mores and play. We humans cannot teach them such things. All of my furry kids that came to me with abuse backgrounds had no concept of play. They were able to learn to play, but it was a direct result of interactions with other furry friends teaching them. Learning takes place by observation and communication just as it does for humans. Animals do communicate with each other. Humans just aren't fluent in their language, and thus we tend to write it off and think they don't have a language. Animals need relationships and bond very deeply. Animals also remember these bonds that they have formed. Love never dies. It is an energy that changes anyone who experiences it. Humans can remember past loves, and animals are no different.

Let me tell you a true story that exemplifies this kind of remembrance. My folks had a dog, Buck, whom they truly loved, especially my pop. Buck was his best friend. When Buck died and went to heaven, my folks were crushed. Losing a loved one brings terrible grief. They didn't want to get another dog. The pain was too much. Well, as God would have it, almost a year later I saw two dogs in my neighborhood that I had never seen before. One of the dogs was a dalmatian; the other one was a mixed breed, reddish-brown in color with a bushy tail. When I went out to see them, they initially wouldn't come near me. They apparently were friends with the neighbor dog, Coco, who was a chocolate lab that lived across the street. Remember how we were talking about how animals need to learn from each other? Here is an example of that. As I said, the two dogs seemed leery of me. Coco, being the smart dog she is, seemed to sense this. She came over to me and seemed to be telling them that I was a safe person and could be trusted. All I know is that after Coco came over to me, the reddish-brown dog came over and then the dalmatian. Communication, communication, communication.

I found no owners for the dogs. I thought that maybe God had brought these two dogs for my folks! I was thrilled. My folks didn't say no, and it seemed that these two had found a good home and my folks had received a blessing from God. This is the story of Hannah and Lucky (Lucky being the dalmatian). Lucky was around five years old. Hannah was around six to seven months. Although we were uncertain how long these two had been traveling together, Lucky and Hannah were very bonded and had a love for each other. With her contrary nature, Hannah became quite a handful for my folks. She wouldn't come when they called her, and they didn't have a fenced yard. She drove my parents crazy with her contrary, opinionated ways. She ended up coming back to live with me.

Lucky had a bit of an attitude problem with my Jonah, so get-togethers with my parents excluded the dogs to maintain peace. Lucky and Hannah didn't see each other for two years. After my mom passed away and went to heaven in 2004, Pop and I decided that we had to address the issue regarding the dogs and that they had to learn to tolerate each other. When Hannah and Lucky saw each other again after two years, it was like two old friends being reunited. They never forgot each other and still had that strong bond. As I said, love never dies. I think it was this bond that helped Lucky and Jonah to finally tolerate each other. Maybe Hannah talked some sense into Lucky. Communication is everything!

Animals need and thrive with good relationships. I can see that when observing my pets. If I have to take one of my dogs to the vet, all the others get upset. When we come home, they are all happy to be back together. When Noah and Jonah need to be groomed (being cocker spaniels, it is a given), I take them together. I know that they will feel more secure being together rather than being alone and faced with all those instruments of beauty. My birds are happy being together and not alone. Even my ducks are bonded with each other. They are usually close to each other in the yard. If one is not with the group, Rosemary (my male mallard) quacks and begins searching for his missing girl.

Look around at other animals and you will see similar bonds. There are horses and cows living next to me. Just watching them, it is easy to see the bonds they have with each other. They stick together. Being separated is not a happy situation. Rabbits run and play with each other. It can be mesmerizing to watch them play. The neighbor dogs across the street got in trouble together because they decided it might be fun to go for a swim in another neighbor's pond. Would one of them have done that by him or herself? Probably not, because everyone knows it is a lot more fun to go on an adventure with a friend rather than by yourself. As I have said, God made us all to have meaningful relationships.

Animals will also help each other out when there is a need. I am sure that you have heard stories of animal moms who have taken on nursing other orphan animals. A cat will nurse other orphan cats. I have heard of a cat nursing baby puppies. I even saw on one of those animal TV shows where a Doberman cared for little baby rabbits. Animals, unlike us humans, seem to see that we are all in this together. Differences don't seem to matter in a time of need. I found a nest of baby cardinals just outside the rabbits' room window. When I was in the rabbits' room giving them fresh greens for dinner, I heard the birds chirping frantically. I looked out and saw a snake slithering up the bush to get the baby cardinals. I ran outside to help them. I noticed that a lot of birds were coming to the rescue, attempting to distract and scare the snake away. The birds included the parent cardinals but also a multitude of other birds. They might not have been their babies, but they knew a neighbor in need and offered their assistance. The snake was taken care of, saving the babies, but the response of all the neighboring birds is something to be commended.

When you have relationships and love deeply, you inevitably will be faced with grief when a loved one dies. Humans understand the overwhelming grief when losing someone. Those of you who have had a dear, beloved pet understand the awful pain felt when he or she dies. Animals feel that pain and grief too. All creatures go through a time of mourning. When Ashley, my cocker, was near death, Albert had a very hard time dealing with it. He loved Ashley deeply. He obviously knew what was coming and, in his way, tried to avoid it. Toward the end, he didn't even come around Ashley much. I think it was too hard for him. Some might say how awful that is, but be truthful—many humans react the same way when faced with death. I made a huge mistake after Ashley died. I allowed Albert to be outside for the burial. He was a mess after that for a long time. He didn't want to go outside and would definitely avoid the area where she was buried. He knew what was going on, and it bothered him immensely. I learned the hard way to never allow any of my kids out during the burial ceremony. We grieve our way. They grieve their way. When Albert passed away in my home, Noah was right beside the bed. He mourned, but he dealt with it differently. I guess he wanted to be there close to Albert through the end of his life here on earth.

I came home from work one day to a horrid sight. A hawk had killed one of my ducks and was eating her. Of course, I got the hawk to leave, crying terribly, and truth be known, saying some awful words to that hawk. My other ducks were huddled together by the barn, scared to death and traumatized. It took time for them to get through that terrible event. To this day, they can spot a hawk a mile away and take shelter. I have lost other ducks at different times. Each time, the other ducks were far away from the deceased duck and remained extremely solemn. They knew what had happened and felt grief and pain.

My parakeet, Rosalinda, chirped out a cry I had never heard before one early morning. I went in to see what was wrong. Billy, my other parakeet, lay on the floor of their cage. She had just passed away into heaven. When I removed her from the cage, she was still warm. Rosalinda cried out at the moment of her passing. When my gerbil, Jake, died, Ansel, my other gerbil, grieved so badly that within a week he died as well. I was faced with making the awful decision that I needed to put my rabbit, Clover, to sleep. She had suffered from abscesses, and in spite of all the medical intervention, she wasn't getting better and was in terrible pain. After doing what was best for Clover, which was definitely an excruciating decision to make, I was told to bring my deceased Clover home to allow the other rabbits to see her. It would help with their grief process. The vet knew that rabbits have their own way of grieving. Driving to work one early morning, I saw a dead deer in the road that had apparently been hit by a car. There was another deer standing in the median looking at his or her friend, grief stricken. Another time I saw a dead dog on the side of the road right by a house. Another dog was sitting by the dead dog, not leaving his side. Animals have feelings just like us. They grieve deeply just like we do. They go through the cycle of life just like humans.

We have touched on many aspects of psychosocial development in animals in this chapter. I have given numerous examples to help clarify this message. Each creature has its own unique soul that God breathed into him or her. Every creature experiences life with a wide array of feelings; with a desire and need to have its basic needs met; and with the need to feel safe, secure, and that they belong, including experiencing love from family and friends. Animals have feelings too. Animals are like sponges and soak up the energy that is in their environment, whether it is positive or negative. They suffer in abusive situations and flourish in nurturing environments. They develop and thrive with meaningful relationships and experience grief when a relationship is severed.

Let us reflect on all the scriptures that we have read in this book. God put humans here on Planet Earth to care for His creation and all of His beautiful creatures that He made. God has provided multiple instructions about how we should be kind and loving to His creatures and provide for their needs. He has repeated these instructions over and over and over again. Shouldn't we heed God's call and be good stewards of what He has put us in charge of? Don't we really have an immense responsibility to God to be the good caretakers of His creation, which is the job He designed all of us to take?

I hope this has given you some things to think about. My wish and hope is that everyone reading this may become a bit more mindful and thoughtful regarding animals and their needs. God put us in charge as caretakers over His creatures both in our homes and throughout the world. So when we see an animal in need, please let us not just turn away and do nothing. They are God's creatures and deserve more compassion and respect than that. Let us all be like the Good Samaritan and help out our fellow creatures, because we are *all* neighbors here on Planet Earth.

Conclusion

Come, Let Us Reason Together

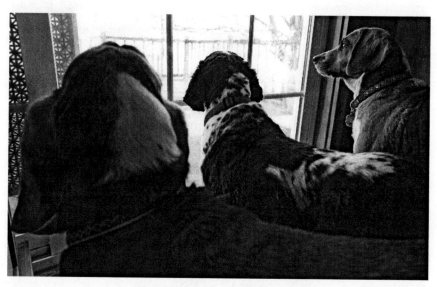

photo taken by Suzy Mast-Lee

I have to tell you this journey has been an incredible ride. When I
started out so many years ago, I had no idea for sure where I would end
up. It was stepping out into a completely unknown territory. I wasn't
sure what I would find about God's views regarding animals and His
purpose for them. I only knew that I needed to find out no matter what.

What I ended up discovering was overwhelming. There is so much on the subject, as you can see. And remember that I couldn't include all the scriptures due to quantity. I am also baffled about the fact that there has been a lot of propaganda to the contrary. Very sad. We need to be very careful about false teachers.

When I initially started out on this journey to find out the truth about God's real plan concerning animals, I had a hard time finding much information from other sources. As I stated earlier, I found a couple of books and numerous articles off the Internet, but I have to say that as time went on, I did find more on the subject. There are books written about this matter, although it is very difficult to get your hands on them. I was pleasantly surprised to find that there have been famous theologians whom I am sure were quite knowledgeable about the Bible who also saw what I saw in the word of God. John Wesley, founder of the Methodist Church, wrote an entire sermon on the matter, "The General Deliverance," which I highly recommend reading and have included a copy of as an appendix. John Wesley uses scriptures from Romans chapter 8 for the backbone of his sermon. I shared this scripture in the chapter "The Bridge":

"For the earnest expectation of the creature waiteth for the manifestation of the sons of God. For the creature was made subject to vanity, not willingly, but by reason of him who hath subjected the same in hope, because the creature itself also shall be delivered from the bondage of corruption into the glorious liberty of the children of God. For we know that the whole creation groaneth and travaileth in pain until now" (Romans 8:19–22, KJV).

Mary Buddemeyer-Porter uses this same scripture in her book, *Will I See Fido in Heaven? Scripturally Revealing God's Eternal Plan for His Lesser Creatures.* When I read that scripture for the first time, I cried with

Animals as Seen Through God's Eyes

elation. Wesley reflects on Isaiah 11:6–9 and the peaceable kingdom as a picture of how heaven will be, which will include all animals living peacefully together. I also found it quite interesting that he became vegetarian.

St. Francis of Assisi was noted for caring and preaching to the animals. St. Francis took our Lord's command very seriously when Jesus said, "And he said unto them, Go ye into all the world, and preach the gospel to every creature" (Mark 16:15, KJV).

St. Francis would even refer to the animals and birds as his brothers and sisters. Even C. S. Lewis knew that animals were much more significant in God's eyes than most humans thought. Apparently he was somewhat concerned about speaking up on his beliefs for fear of being ridiculed by others. When I read *The Chronicles of Narnia,* even though it is a children's fiction series, it is very evident that he interweaves his beliefs that God plans to redeem all of His creation.

In this book we started out back at the Garden of Eden. We looked at what God's initial plan was for humans and all His creation. Next we explored the downfall of mankind as a result of sin, and the effects on all creation. We journeyed on to look at what happened after the Garden of Eden and God's redeeming love. We looked at verses and psalms that share how all creation praises and worships God and how His loving care extends to all of His creation. Due to the sin factor, relationships changed. We explored the impact of these changes. God continued to reach out to point us in the right direction. There are countless stories and principles to give us wisdom on how to live. In these examples, God used animals as illustrations or to help educate us on what good character is all about. He gave countless examples of how we should treat His creatures and what our responsibilities are regarding them.

I included these because if God saw that this was so important to include it in the Bible, I think we definitely need to pay attention. Next we explored how man tried to get right with God and looked at the purpose of sacrifices. Man missed the entire meaning behind sacrifice, and it became a ritual instead of humbling yourself before God. God sent His prophets to share what He really wanted, but very few listened. We saw how God Himself came down to earth in human form as Jesus Christ to make the ultimate sacrifice and bring all things (creatures and creation itself) back to Him. He paid the ultimate price for sin and to make a new way. And finally we got a glimpse of heaven. We traveled full circle. God always does things completely.

Come, let us reason together. Let us truly look at the facts of the matter and what God says about all of God's creatures and His plan for all things. God is a much bigger God than any of us can even imagine. His ways go way beyond our ways. His thoughts are far greater than our thoughts. We have traveled through the Bible from Genesis to Revelation. God's word doesn't change. It remains consistent throughout. Humans are the ones who sinned. They wanted all the glamour and the glory but didn't want the responsibility and commitment. Animals didn't sin. They know who they are in God. Although all creatures have changed from their original state due to humans' sin and wickedness, they still look to God for their help. God tries to teach us how we should treat our fellow creatures, how to be good caretakers of God's creation. God has made attempts over and over to get our attention and share His expectations. God has beckoned us to see His big picture of His grand plan. He has promised a covenant He will make with people and His creatures to make peace throughout and have the knowledge of the Lord cover all the land as the waters cover the sea. God came down to earth in the form of man to sacrifice Himself once and for all for sin and to redeem all creation, bringing everything to Himself. What Jesus Christ did for mankind He did for His entire creation. We have seen a glimpse of heaven revealed in the scriptures, which irrefutably show animals and humans living together in a peaceable coexistence.

I am totally and utterly convinced that I will indeed see all of my furry and feathery babies in heaven. There is not a shadow of doubt in my mind. I believe God, and I believe His word, the Bible. As I stated at the beginning of this journey, everyone has a right to believe whatever he or she wants to believe, but just because you believe in something doesn't necessarily make it the truth. I would rather go for the truth. The truth is solid and unshakable.

A scripture that I hold close and that has helped me through this voyage of mine is the middle verse of the Bible: "It is better to trust in the Lord than to put confidence in man" (Psalm 118:8, KJV). I believe there is sound reason why this verse is the exact middle verse in the Bible. It is the heart of everything. We can't just pick and choose what we want to believe from the Bible and leave the rest. God is either truthful or He is a liar. He cannot be both. Either the Bible is truthful and the word of God or it isn't.

I have completed the task God has given me to do. I have thoroughly researched the matter and shared with you my findings. What I have shared comes straight from the scriptures. There are countless more scriptures in the Bible on this subject that I didn't include because the quantity is so great. Nowhere could I find that it says animals don't have souls. In fact, I found overwhelming evidence to the contrary. I challenge you to thoughtfully look over the evidence, read the Bible for yourself, pray to God for the truth to be revealed to you, and ask Him what He wants you to do with it. The torch has been passed.

Appendix

John Wesley

Sermon 60

[text of the 1872 edition]

The General Deliverance

The earnest expectation of the creature waiteth for the manifestation of the sons of God. For the creature was made subject to vanity, not willingly, but by reason of him that subjected it: Yet in hope that the creature itself also shall be delivered from the bondage of corruption, into the glorious liberty of the sons of God. For we know that the whole creation groaneth and travaileth in pain together until now.

—Rom. 8: 19–22.

Nothing is more sure, than that as "the Lord is loving to every man," so "his mercy is over all his works;" all that have sense, all that are capable of pleasure or pain, of happiness or misery. In consequence of this, "He openeth his hand, and filleth all things living with plenteousness. He prepareth food for cattle, "as well as "herbs for the children of men." He provideth for the fowls of the air, "feeding the young ravens when they cry unto him." "He sendeth the springs into the rivers, that run among the hills, to give drink to every beast of the field," and that even "the wild asses may quench their thirst." And, suitably to this, he directs us to be tender of even the meaner creatures; to show mercy to these also. "Thou shalt not muzzle the ox that treadeth out the corn." —A custom which is observed in the eastern countries even to this day. And this is by no means contradicted by St. Paul's question: "Doth God take care of oxen?" Without doubt he does. We cannot deny it, without flatly contradicting his word. The plain meaning of the Apostle is, Is this all that is implied in the text? Hath it not a farther meaning? Does it not teach us, we are to feed the bodies of those whom we desire to feed our souls? Meantime it is certain, God "giveth grass for the cattle," as well as "herbs for the use of men."

But how are these Scriptures reconcilable to the present state of things? How are they consistent with what we daily see round about us, in every part of the creation? If the Creator and Father of every living thing is rich in mercy towards all; if he does not overlook or despise any of the works of his own hands; if he wills even the meanest of them to be happy, according to their degree; how comes it to pass, that such a complication of evils oppresses, yea, overwhelms them? How is it that misery of all kinds over spreads the face of the earth? This is a question which has puzzled the wisest philosophers in all ages: And it cannot be answered without having recourse to the oracles of God. But, taking these for our guide we may inquire,

I. What was the original state of the brute creation?

II. In what state is it at present? And,

III. In what state will it be at the manifestation of the children of God?

I. 1. We may inquire, in the First place, What was the original state of the brute creation?

And may we not learn this, even from the place which was assigned them; namely, the garden of God? All the beasts of the field, and all the fowls of the air, were with Adam in paradise. And there is no question but their state was suited to their place: It was paradisiacal; perfectly happy. Undoubtedly it bore a near resemblance to the state of man himself. By taking, therefore, a short view of the one, we may conceive the other. Now, "man was made in the image of God." But "God is a Spirit:" So therefore was man. (Only that spirit, being designed to dwell on earth, was lodged in an earthly tabernacle.) As such, he had an innate principle of self-motion. And so, it seems, has every spirit in the universe; this being the proper distinguishing difference between spirit and matter, which is totally, essentially passive and inactive, as appears from a thousand experiments. He was, after the likeness of his Creator, endued with understanding; a capacity of apprehending whatever objects were brought before it, and of judging concerning them. He was endued with a will, exerting itself in various affections and passions: And, lastly, with liberty, or freedom of choice; without which all the rest would have been in vain, and he would have been no more capable of serving his Creator than a piece of earth or marble; he would have been as incapable of vice or virtue, as any part of the inanimate creation. In these, in the power of self-motion, understanding, will, and liberty, the natural image of God consisted.

2. How far his power of self-motion then extended, it is impossible for us to determine. It is probable, that he had a far higher degree both of

swiftness and strength, than any of his posterity ever had, and much less any of the lower creatures. It is certain, he had such strength of understanding as no man ever since had. His understanding was perfect in its kind; capable of apprehending all things clearly, and judging concerning them according to truth, without any mixture of error. His will had no wrong bias of any sort; but all his passions and affections were regular, Being steadily and uniformly guided by the dictates of his unerring understanding; embracing nothing but good, and every good in proportion to its degree of intrinsic goodness. His liberty likewise was wholly guided by his understanding: He chose, or refused, according to its direction. Above all, (which was his highest excellence, far more valuable than all the rest put together,) he was a creature capable of God; capable of knowing, loving, and obeying his Creator. And, in fact, he did know God, did unfeignedly love and uniformly obey him. This was the supreme perfection of man; (as it is of all intelligent beings;) the continually seeing, and loving, and obeying the Father of the spirits of all flesh. From this right state and right use of all his faculties, his happiness naturally flowed. In this the essence of his happiness consisted; But it was increased by all the things that were round about him. He saw, with unspeakable pleasure, the order, the beauty, the harmony, of all the creatures; of all animated, all inanimate nature; the serenity of the skies; the sun walking in brightness; the sweetly variegated clothing of the earth; the trees, the fruits, the flowers, And liquid lapse of murmuring streams.

Nor was this pleasure interrupted by evil of any kind. It had no alloy of sorrow or pain, whether of body or mind. For while he was innocent he was impassive; incapable of suffering. Nothing could stain his purity of joy. And, to crown all, he was immortal.

3. To this creature, endured with all these excellent faculties, thus qualified for his high charge, God said, "Have thou dominion over the

fish of the sea, and over the fowl of the air, and over every living thing that moveth upon the earth." (Gen. 1: 28) And so the Psalmist: "Thou madest him to have dominion over the works of thy hands: Thou hast put all things under his feet: All sheep and oxen, yea, and the beasts of the field, the fowl of the air, and the fish of the sea, and whatsoever passeth through the paths of the seas." (Psalm 8: 6, &c.) So that man was God's vicegerent upon earth, the prince and governor of this lower world; and all the blessings of God flowed through him to the inferior creatures. Man was the channel of conveyance between his Creator and the whole brute creation.

4. But what blessings were those that were then conveyed through man to the lower creatures? What was the original state of the brute creatures, when they were first created?

This deserves a more attentive consideration than has been usually given it. It is certain these, as well as man, had an innate principle of self-motion; and that, at least, in as high a degree as they enjoy it at this day. Again: They were endued with a degree of understanding; not less than that they are possessed of now. They had also a will, including various passions, which, likewise, they still enjoy: And they had liberty, a power of choice; a degree of which is still found in every living creature. Nor can we doubt but their understanding too was, in the beginning, perfect in its kind. Their passions and affections were regular, and their choice always guided by their understanding.

5. What then is the barrier between men and brutes? the line which they cannot pass? It was not reason. Set aside that ambiguous term: Exchange it for the plain word, understanding: and who can deny that brutes have this? We may as well deny that they have sight or hearing. But it is this: Man is capable of God; the inferior creatures are not.

We have no ground to believe that they are, in any degree, capable of knowing, loving, or obeying God. This is the specific difference between man and brute; the great gulf which they cannot pass over. And as a loving obedience to God was the perfection of man, so a loving obedience to man was the perfection of brutes. And as long as they continued in this, they were happy after their kind; happy in the right state and the right use of their respective faculties. Yea, and so long they had some shadowy resemblance of even moral goodness. For they had gratitude to man for benefits received, and a reverence for him.

They had likewise a kind of benevolence to each other, unmixed with any contrary temper.

How beautiful many of them were, we may conjecture from that which still remains; and that not only in the noblest creatures, but in those of the lowest order. And they were all surrounded, not only with plenteous food, but with every thing that could give them pleasure; pleasure unmixed with pain; for pain was not yet; it had not entered into paradise.

And they too were immortal: For "God made not death; neither hath he pleasure in the death of any living."

6. How true then is that word, "God saw everything that he had made: and behold it was very good!" But how far is this from being the present case! In what a condition is the whole lower world!—to say nothing of inanimate nature, wherein all the elements seem to be out of course, and by turns to fight against man. Since man rebelled against his Maker, in what a state is all animated nature! Well might the Apostle say of this: "The whole creation groaneth and travaileth together in pain until now." This directly refers to the brute creation. In what state this is at present we are now to consider.

II. 1. As all the blessings of God in paradise flowed through man to the inferior creatures; as man was the great channel of communication, between the Creator and the whole brute creation; so when man made himself incapable of transmitting those blessings, that communication was necessarily cut off. The intercourse between God and the inferior creatures being stopped, those blessings could no longer flow in upon them. And then it was that "creature," every creature, "was subjected to vanity," to sorrow, to pain of every kind, to all manner of evils: Not, indeed, "willingly," not by its own choice, not by any act or deed of its own; "but by reason of Him that subjected it," by the wise permission of God, determining to draw eternal good out of this temporary evil.

2. But in what respect was "the creature," every creature, then "made subject to vanity?"

What did the meaner creatures suffer, when man rebelled against God? It is probable they sustained much loss, even in the lower faculties; their vigour, strength, and swiftness. But undoubtedly they suffered far more in their understanding; more than we can easily conceive. Perhaps insects and worms had then as much understanding as the most intelligent brutes have now: Whereas millions of creatures have, at present, little more understanding than the earth on which they crawl, or the rock to which they adhere. They suffered still more in their will, in their passions; which were then variously distorted, and frequently set in flat opposition to the little understanding that was left them. Their liberty, likewise, was greatly impaired; yea, in many cases, totally destroyed. They are still utterly enslaved to irrational appetites, which have the full dominion over them. The very foundations of their nature are out of course; are turned upside down. As man is deprived of *his* perfection, his loving obedience to God; so brutes are deprived of *their* perfection, their loving obedience to man. The far greater part of them flee from him; studiously avoid his hated presence. The most of the rest set him at open defiance; yea, destroy him, if it be in their power. A few only, those we commonly term domestic animals, retain more or less of their original disposition, (through the mercy of God,) love him still, and pay obedience to him.

3. Setting these few aside, how little shadow of good, of gratitude, of benevolence, of any right temper, is now to be found in any part of the brute creation! On the contrary, what savage fierceness, what unrelenting cruelty; are invariably observed in thousands of creatures; yea, is inseparable from their natures! Is it only the lion, the tiger, the wolf, among the inhabitants of the forest and plains—the shark, and a few more voracious monsters, among the inhabitants of the waters,—or the eagle, among birds,—that tears the flesh, sucks the blood, and crushes the bones of their helpless fellow-creatures? Nay; the harmless fly, the laborious ant, the painted butterfly, are treated in the same merciless manner, even by the innocent songsters of the grove! The innumerable tribes of poor insects are continually devoured by them. And whereas there is but a small number, comparatively, of beasts of prey on the earth, it is quite otherwise in the liquid element.

There are but few inhabitants of the waters, whether of the sea, or of the rivers, which do not devour whatsoever they can master: Yea, they exceed herein all the beasts of the forest, and all the birds of prey. For none of these have been ever observed to prey upon their own species:

Saevis inter se convenit ursis:

Even savage bears will not each other tear.

But the water-savages swallow up all, even of their own kind, that are smaller and weaker than themselves. Yea, such, at present, is the miserable constitution of the world, to such vanity is it now subjected, that an immense majority of creatures, perhaps a million to one, can no otherwise preserve their own lives, than by destroying their fellow-creatures!

4. And is not the very form, the outward appearance, of many of the creatures, as horrid as their dispositions? Where is the beauty which was stamped upon them when they came first out of the hands of their Creator? There is not the least trace of it left: So far from it, that they are shocking to behold! Nay, they are not only terrible and grisly to look upon, but deformed, and that to a high degree. Yet their features, ugly as they are at best, are frequently made more deformed than usual, when they are distorted by pain; which they cannot avoid, any more than the wretched sons of men. Pain of various kinds, weakness, sickness, diseases innumerable, come upon them; perhaps from within; perhaps from one another; perhaps from the inclemency of seasons; from fire, hail, snow, or storm; or from a thousand causes which they cannot foresee or prevent.

5. Thus, "as by one man sin entered into the world, and death by sin; even so death passed upon all men;" and not on man only, but on those creatures also that "did not sin after the similitude of Adam's transgression." And not death alone came upon them, but all of its train of preparatory evils; pain, and ten thousand sufferings. Nor these only, but likewise all those irregular passions, all those unlovely tempers, (which in men are sins, and even in the brutes are sources of misery,) "passed upon all" the inhabitants of the earth; and remain in all, except the children of God.

6. During this season of vanity, not only the feebler creatures are continually destroyed by the stronger; not only the strong are frequently

destroyed by those that are of equal strength; but both the one and the other are exposed to the violence and cruelty of him that is now their common enemy,—man. And if his swiftness or strength is not equal to theirs, yet his art more than supplies that defect. By this he eludes all their force, how great so ever it be; by this he defeats all their swiftness; and, notwithstanding their various shifts and contrivances, discovers all their retreats. He pursues them over the widest plains, and through the thickest forests. He overtakes them in the fields of air, he finds them out in the depths of the sea. Nor are the mild and friendly creatures who still own his sway, and are duteous to his commands, secured thereby from more than brutal violence; from outrage and abuse of various kinds. Is the generous horse, that serves his master's necessity or pleasure with unwearied diligence,—is the faithful dog, that waits the motion of his hand, or his eye, exempt from this? What returns for their long and faithful service do many of these poor creatures find? And what a dreadful difference is there, between what they suffer from their fellow-brutes, and what they suffer from the tyrant man! The lion, the tiger, or the shark, gives them pain from mere necessity, in order to prolong their own life; and puts them out of their pain at once: But the human shark, without any such necessity, torments them of his free choice; and perhaps continues their lingering pain till, after months or years, death signs their release.

III. 1. But will "the creature," will even the brute creation, always remain in this deplorable condition? God forbid that we should affirm this; yea, or even entertain such a thought!

While "the whole creation groaneth together," (whether men attend or not,) their groans are not dispersed in idle air, but enter into the ears of Him that made them. While his creatures "travail together in pain," he knoweth all their pain, and is bringing them nearer and nearer to the birth, which shall be accomplished in its season. He seeth "the earnest expectation" wherewith the whole animated creation "waiteth for" that final "manifestation of the sons of God;" in which "they themselves also shall be delivered" (not by annihilation; annihilation is not deliverance) "from the" present "bondage of corruption, into" a measure of "glorious liberty of the children of God."

2. Nothing can be more express: Away with vulgar prejudices, and let the plain word of God take place. They "shall be delivered from the bondage of corruption, into glorious liberty,"—even a measure, according as they are capable,—of "the liberty of the children of God."

A general view of this is given us in the twenty-first chapter of the Revelation. When He that "sitteth on the great white throne" hath pronounced, "Behold, I make all things new;" when the word is fulfilled, "The tabernacle of God is with men, and they shall be his people, and God himself shall be with them and be their God;" —then the following blessing shall take place (not only on the children of men; there is no such restriction in the text; but) on every creature according to its capacity: "God shall wipe away all tears from their eyes. And there shall be no more death, neither sorrow, nor crying. Neither shall there be any more pain: For the former things are passed away."

3. To descend to a few particulars: The whole brute creation will then, undoubtedly, be restored, not only to the vigour, strength, and swiftness which they had at their creation, but to a far higher degree of each than they ever enjoyed. The will be restored, not only to that measure of understanding which they had in paradise, but to a degree of it as much higher than that, as the understanding of an elephant is beyond that of a worm. And whatever affections they had in the garden of God, will be restored with vast increase; being exalted and refined in a manner which we ourselves are not now able to comprehend.

The liberty they then had will be completely restored, and they will be free in all their motions. They will be delivered from all irregular appetites, from all unruly passions, from every disposition that is either evil in itself, or has any tendency to evil. No rage will be found in any creature, no fierceness, no cruelty, or thirst for blood. So far from it that "the wolf shall dwell with the lamb, the leopard shall lie down with the kid; the calf and the young lion together; and a little child shall lead them. The cow and the bear shall feed together; and the lion shall eat straw like the ox. They shall not hurt nor destroy in all my holy mountain." (Isaiah 11: 6, & c.)

4. Thus, in that day, all the vanity to which they are now helplessly subject will be abolished; they will suffer no more, either from within or without; the days of their groaning are ended. At the same time, there can be no reasonable doubt, but all the horridness of their appearance, and all the deformity of their aspect, will vanish away, and be exchanged for their primeval beauty. And with their beauty their happiness will return; to which there can then be no obstruction. As there will be nothing within, so there will be nothing without, to give them any uneasiness: No heat or cold, no storm or tempest, but one perennial spring. In the new earth, as well as in the new heavens, there will be nothing to give pain, but everything that the wisdom and goodness of God can create to give happiness. As a recompense for what they once suffered, while under the "bondage of corruption," when God has "renewed the face of the earth," and their corruptible body has put on incorruption, they shall enjoy happiness suited to their state, without alloy, without interruption, and without end.

5. But though I doubt not that the Father of All has a tender regard for even his lowest creatures, and that, in consequence of this, he will make them large amends for all they suffer while under their present

bondage; yet I dare not affirm that he has an *equal regard f*or them and for the children of men. I do not believe that He sees with equal eyes, as Lord of all, A hero perish, or a sparrow fall.

By no means. This is exceeding pretty; but it is absolutely false. For though

Mercy, with truth and endless grace,
O'er all his works doth reign,
Yet chiefly he delights to bless
His favourite creature, man.

God regards his meanest creatures much; but he regards man much more. He does not *equally* regard a hero and a sparrow; the best of men and the lowest of brutes. "How *much more* does your heavenly Father care for you!" says He "who is in the bosom of his Father." Those who thus strain the point, are clearly confuted by his question, "Are not ye m*uch better* than they?" Let it suffice, that God regards everything that he hath made, in its own order, and in proportion to that measure of his own image which he has stamped upon it.

6. May I be permitted to mention here a conjecture concerning the brute creation? What, if it should then please the all-wise, the all-gracious Creator to raise them higher in the scale of beings? What, if it should please him, when he makes us "equal to angels," to make them what we are now,—creatures capable of God; capable of knowing and loving and enjoying the Author of their being? If it should be so, ought our eye to be evil because he is good? However this be, he will certainly do what will be most for his own glory.

7. If it be objected to all this, (as very probably it will,) "But of what use will those creatures be in that future state?" I answer this by another

question, What use are they of now? If there be (as has commonly been supposed) eight thousand species of insects, who is able to inform us of what use seven thousand of them are? If there are four thousand species of fishes, who can tell us of what use are more than three thousand of them? If there are six hundred sorts of birds, who can tell of what use five hundred of those species are? If there be four hundred sorts of beasts, to what use do three hundred of them serve?

Consider this; consider how little we know of even the present designs of God; and then you will not wonder that we know still less of what he designs to do in the new heavens and the new earth.

8. "But what end does it answer to dwell upon this subject, which we so imperfectly understand?" To consider so much as we do understand, so much as God has been pleased to reveal to us, may answer that excellent end—to illustrate that mercy of God which "is over all his works." And it may exceedingly confirm our belief that, much more, he "is loving to every man." For how well may we urge our Lord's words, "Are not ye much better than they?" If, then, the Lord takes such care of the fowls of the air, and of the beasts of the field, shall he not much more take care of *you,* creatures of a nobler order? If "the Lord will save," as the inspired writer affirms, "both man and beast," in their several degrees, surely "the children of men may put their trust under the shadow of his wings!"

9. May it not answer another end; namely, furnish us with a full answer to a plausible objection against the justice of God, in suffering numberless creatures that never had sinned to be so severely punished? They could not sin, for they were not moral agents. Yet how severely do they suffer! – yea, many of them, beasts of burden in particular, almost the whole time of their abode on earth; So that they can have no retribution here below. But the objection vanishes away, if we consider

that something better remains after death for these poor creatures also; that these, likewise, shall one day be delivered from this bondage of corruption, and shall then receive an ample amends for all their present sufferings.

10. One more excellent end may undoubtedly be answered by the preceding considerations.

They may encourage us to imitate Him whose mercy is over all his works. They may soften our hearts toward the meaner creatures, knowing that the Lord careth for them. It may enlarge our hearts towards those poor creatures, to reflect that, as vile as they appear in our eyes, not one of them is forgotten in the sight of our Father which is in heaven.

Through all the vanity to which they are now subjected, let us look to what God hath prepared for them. Yea, let us habituate ourselves to look forward, beyond this present scene of bondage, to the happy time when they will be delivered there from into the liberty of the children of God.

11. From what has been said, I cannot but draw one inference, which no man of reason can deny. If it is this which distinguishes men from beasts,—that they are creatures capable of God, capable of knowing and loving and enjoying him; then whoever is "without God in the world," whoever does not know or love or enjoy God, and is not careful about the matter, does, in effect, disclaim the nature of man, and degrade himself into a beast. Let such vouchsafe a little attention to those remarkable words of Solomon: "I said in my heart concerning the estate of the sons of men,—They might see that they themselves are beasts." (Eccles. 3: 18) These sons of men are undoubtedly beasts; and that by their own act and deed; for they deliberately and willfully disclaim the sole characteristic of human nature. It is true, they may have a share

of reason; they have speech, and they walk erect; but they have not the mark, the only mark, which totally separates man from the brute creation. "That which befalleth beasts, the same thing befalleth them." They are equally without God in the world; "so that a man" of this kind "hath no pre-eminence above a beast."

12. So much more let all those who are of a nobler turn of mind assert the distinguishing dignity of their nature. Let all who are of a more generous spirit know and maintain their rank in the scale of beings. Rest not till you enjoy the privilege of humanity—the knowledge and love of God. Lift up your heads, ye creature capable of God! Lift up your hearts to the Source of your being!

Know God, and teach your souls to know
The joys that from religion flow.

Give your hearts to Him who, together with ten thousand blessings, has given you his Son, his only Son! Let your continual "fellowship be with the Father, and with his Son, Jesus Christ!" Let God be in all your thoughts, and ye will be men indeed. Let him be your God and your All,—the desire of your eyes, the joy of your heart, and your portion for ever.

Bibliography

Buddemeyer-Porter, Mary. *Will I See Fido in Heaven? Scripturally Revealing God's Eternal Plan for His Lesser Creatures.* Manchester, Missouri: Eden Publications, 2000.

Canfield, Jack, Mark Victor Hanson, Marty Becker, D.V.M., and Carol Kline. *Chicken Soup for the Pet Lover's Soul.* Deerfield Beach, Florida: Health Communications, Inc., 1998.

Francis of Assisi. "Sermon to the Birds." The History Place. Accessed June 23, 2006. http://www.historyplace.com/speeches/saintfran.htm

Francis of Assisi. "Prayer for Animals." MyCatholicSource.com. Accessed April 7, 2014. http://www.mycatholicsource.com/mcs/pc/saint_francis_section_prayers.htm

Gronowicz, Antoni. *God's Broker: The Life of John Paul II.* New York: Richardson & Snyder, 1984.

Liardon, Robert. *God's Generals II: The Roaring Reformers.* New Kensington, PA: Whitaker House, 2003.

Randour, Mary Lou. *Animal Grace: Entering a Spiritual Relationship with Our Fellow Creatures.* Novato, CA: New World Library, 2000.

Shires, H. and Parker, P. "The Book of Deuteronomy." In *The Interpreter's Bible, Vol. II,* edited by W. R. Bowie, P. Scherer, J. Knox, S. Terrien, and N. B. Harmon, 463–479. Nashville: Abingdon-Cokesbury Press, 1953.

Tompkins, Ptolemy. "Do Pets Go to Heaven?" *Guideposts* (February 2005): 86–92.

Wesley, John. "The General Deliverance." Rapture Ready. Accessed June 7, 2006. http://www.raptureme.com/resource/wesley/serm-060.html.

CPSIA information can be obtained at www.ICGtesting.com
Printed in the USA
LVOW06s1326161114

413968LV00001B/296/P